This book is based upon a new discovery about the effect of sound upon the brain. Sound Therapy is a listening technique using high frequency music for beneficially recharging the cortex of the brain. The effect upon the person is one of vitalizing, harmonizing and healing in almost every area of being.

The technique is safe and thoroughly tested. It is simple to do, using a Sony Walkman and the specially recorded cassettes of classical music. These are pleasant to listen to and do not require concentration. The sound can be absorbed at very low volume in the course of all usual activities, taking no time at all from the daily routine.

Documented results include:

- Easier, more efficient sleep. Sleeping time shortened by 2 - 3 hours a night.
- New vitality and sense of well-being.
- Obliteration of tiredness
- Deep relaxation and relief of anxiety, with consequent healing of stress-related disorders such as high blood pressure, hypertension, digestive problems.
- Improved hearing, restoration of hearing loss due to aging.
- Curing of disorders stemming from imbalance of inner ear fluid: nausea, dizziness, tinnitus.
- Alleviation of stammering and other speech defects.
- Help for dyslexia, hyperactivity and behavioural problems in children.
- Weight loss. Slowing of metabolism and easing of stress act as a natural appetite suppressant.
- Heightened creativity and mental capacity. Improvement of memory, concentration and learning ability.

Sound Therapy
For The Walk Man

by Patricia Joudry

Copyright © 1984
Patricia Joudry

iv

Published by
Steele and Steele
P. O. Box 616
Dalmeny, SASK. SOK 1EO
Canada

ISBN 0-9691687-0-5

Cover Photograph by Courtney Milne

"Sony" and "Walkman" are registered trademarks
of Sony Corporation, Tokyo, Japan.

First printing: June, 1984
Second printing: November, 1984
Third printing, revised: July, 1985
Fourth printing, revised: September, 1986
Fifth printing, revised: May, 1988

10-89

Printed by St. Peter's Press, Muenster, Sask.

v

Other books by Patricia Joudry

Novels

The Dweller on the Threshold
The Selena Tree

Autobiography

And the Children Played
Spirit River to Angels' Roost

Plays

Teach Me How To Cry
The Song of Louise in the Morning
Think Again
The Sand Castle
A Very Modest Orgy
O Listen!
The Conjurer

Metaphysical

Twin Souls

Non fiction

The P.A.N. Environment
(Protected Against Noise)

Chapters

Foreword

I was fascinated by this book, which I read between dawn and breakfast in one sitting! I am prepared to believe that the therapy is a very valuable form of rehabilitation affecting more than the brain, important though that is. It also substantiates the value and use of music.

Music is the voice of the universe, it is the voice of humanity and is part of our existence. Good music is the harmonization of all the vibrations of which matter consists, and it restores us to ourselves and to our universe. It is the bond that we have between our own frequencies and those frequencies which vibrate millions of light years away.

When we hear music we are actually vibrating with the whole audience, and with the performer, and we are thereby put in touch with the composer's mind and heart

I have always felt that music is basically therapeutic, restoring proportions which are squeezed out of shape by the pressures of the day. In a state of physical disequilibrium of the nerves or the mind, music can reach our subconscious and put things in place. And now this therapy is exploring a fascinating new approach to the inner human being. It comes at a time when we are literally being deafened by the rising noise level in our world. The decibel volume is growing with every year and is destroying our hearing and deadening us to our environment.

We seem to think that the ear is dispensable. We concentrate overwhelmingly on what is visual. Everything that we cultivate or build impresses through the eyes, by size and colour and shape. We ignore the miracle of the ear, which conveys images that are far deeper, more subtle and more penetrating than the eye. Light bounces off surfaces and conveys its message through a greater abstraction than sound. Sound goes directly into our bodies. What the aural can do to the inside of our brain, to the "within" of our lives, nothing else can do.

The use of the higher vibrations, as described in this book, opens a whole new world to us. Sound Therapy has a specific effect which seems to have wide implications and to yield undreamed of results. I believe that it constitutes a breakthrough to a new level of effectiveness in music and health.

Yehudi Menuhin

Chapter One

The Sound Effect

It's called Audio-Psycho-Phonology but don't let that scare you. Like all great discoveries it is simple. The brain is recharged by means of sound, releasing latent vitality, obliterating tiredness, heightening mental powers, lessening the need for sleep, and inducing a permanent state of peace and relaxation.

It is a therapy, but you needn't be ill. Known generally as Sound Therapy, it makes the healthy healthier, while healing an array of ills almost as varied as the brain itself. The sound is the music of Mozart, Haydn, Bach and other classical composers, recorded by a special high frequency technique, and the method is the Sony Walkman.

You listen while walking, or reading, driving, shopping, riding the subway or plane, talking, even sleeping. If you're a student you listen and benefit while studying, if you're a monk, while praying, if an artist, while writing or painting.

Until recently Sound Therapy has been used only for the treatment of disorders. The principles were evolved by Dr. A. A. Tomatis of Paris, a former ear, nose and throat specialist whose investigations into the effect of sound upon the human mind have brought him high honour and recognition. The therapy has been used in Europe for more than three decades, achieving dramatic success with deafness, emotional disturbance, hypertension, insomnia, speech defects, epilepsy, hyperactivity, dyslexia, and even autism. Essentially, the treatment consists of listening, through headphones, to high frequency music recorded through a device of Tomatis's invention known as the Electronic Ear. The music is called 'filtered', because the low frequencies have been filtered out, leaving only the highs, or recharging sounds.

The cost in time and money has limited the benefit so far to those in urgent need, the patient being required to sit for several hours a day connected by headphones to the highly sophisticated equipment in the therapist's listening room. There, the filtered music was relayed via reel-to-reel tapes played through the Electronic Ear. Now a way has been found to put the sound program on cassettes. As the effect is dependent upon frequency level, the cassettes must be played on good quality equipment, that is, a tape deck or portable cassette player with a frequency response of 15,000 hertz or upward.

The essential value of the cassette system is the freedom of movement it affords, and thus the great saving in time. Emphasis therefore is laid upon the portable player. The best of these is the Sony Walkman. Sony originated the portable, and there is no other on the market with a higher frequency response than the Walkman. This superb little machine makes Sound Therapy available to the majority, which means the healthy, more or less. Every one of us is subject to stresses. Now, instead of reaching for the valium or the scotch — or somebody's throat — we can reach for the headphones and find calm as well as resurgent energy. Paradoxically, this restorative sound vitalizes while it relaxes. Working directly upon the cortex of the brain, it mobilizes the complementary forces of the human system and provides a natural high and a natural sedative, each coming into play at the dictate of the will.

Each person is a centre of energy, continually influenced by other energies, light and colour and sound. Of these, the most powerful is sound. Poets and mystics speak of the music of the spheres, and we know that the universe is created upon mathematical principles and that mathematics and music have the same root. Some theologians believe that the statement, 'In the beginning was the Word' points to sound as the first creative principle. For once they are not divided from the scientists who claim it all began with a big bang. Maybe it will end with one too, as a demonstration of the difference between sound and noise.

Noise is unwanted sound and is the curse of our day. The populations of entire countries are in danger of suffering hearing losses due to the increasing mechanization of society. The ear, the most sensitive organ in human or animal, is the first to respond to its surroundings. Anyone who has watched a mouse be subjected for a few seconds to the sound of a siren and subsequently suffer a convulsive audiogenic attack that can be fatal, understands that noise is not merely an unpleasant sensation or a danger for the structure of the ear; it is the most important factor in disequilibrium, the great poison that intoxicates the nerve centres at the base of the brain.

Prolonged exposure to noise of 85 decibels or higher produces permanent hearing loss, and traffic noises at the 90 db level are common for the city dweller. Subways and airports have noise levels of 93 and 130 db respectively. One motorcycle generates the same sound hazard as 100 automobiles.

We are passive victims of this noise. There is no protection except to stay in bed with a pillow over our head. The best that the medical profession can do for us is hand out advice like: "Noise-induced hearing loss can be limited by the wearing of ear plugs, by periodic audiometric examination to detect early changes in hearing acuity" (then what?) "and by the environmental control of noise." Have you tried controlling noise in your environment lately? Throwing a shoe out the window at a motorcycle is about the extent of our power.

Now at last it is possible to select the influence to which we want to expose our ear and brain. The noise of the world can't be drowned out, but it can be defused by a gentle sound that we may carry with us anywhere. The high frequency music not only protects the hearing, but in very many cases, where there has not been significant damage to the nerves themselves, has restored hearing already lost. Deterioration usually begins with the sensory hair cells in the basal portion of the cochlea which reduces sensitivity to the higher frequencies first; and that is the area which is rehabilitated by the listening therapy.

The self therapy requires nothing more than that we

listen for a period each day to the cassettes of pleasant, specially processed classical music. We needn't even listen consciously, but can set the Walkman at low volume and go on with whatever we're doing. The effect is of a recharge to the brain, resulting in a release of energy throughout the body.

Tomatis's great contribution to science was to define the role that the ear plays in relation to the human body. He tells us that the ear is made not only for hearing, but is intended to benefit the organism by the stimulation of sound. It can be shown by electroencephalography that the brain uses energy. This electricity is engendered by the central grey nuclei, which are like batteries constantly recharging. The energy which is discharged can be captured. These outbursts of activity do not arise from metabolic processes but from the stimulation of this area by the external input. The battery is recharged via the ear. There are 24,600 sensory cells on the level of the basilar membrane's organ of corti, and these cells are accumulated particularly in the zone of the high frequencies. If one augments the capacity of recharging, via auditory input at high frequencies, the richest area of the basilar membrane is stimulated, as these special nuclei of the cortex are the ones which are more energy laden.

It is not simply a matter of exposing the ear to high frequencies. We are not accustomed to tuning in to these frequencies and won't be capable of filtered-music recharge until the doors leading to the inner ear are opened. A re-education of the middle ear is required, and for this purpose the music is recorded through Tomatis's Electronic Ear.

This complex machine constitutes the essence of the treatment. The device uses filters, affecting selectively bass and treble sounds. There are two filter systems, the bottom set at maximum bass and minimum treble, the top system being the reverse. (The best thing about this is that you don't have to understand it for it to work.) The input can go through only one channel at a time. One channel relaxes the middle ear muscles and the other stimulates them. The passage from one channel to another is regulated by an electronic gate, which opens and closes according to the intensity of sound, creating a rocking motion. The pattern of tension and relaxation acts as a gymnastic and conditions the musculature so that later it will have the ability to regulate the action itself. Faithful perception of sound will become habitual. The ear will have discovered its full listening function and its power to vitalize the brain.

As sound is transformed into nervous influx the charge of energy to the cortex is distributed throughout the nervous system, imparting greater dynamism to the person and flowing into all the areas of need. Like the healing energy of the flesh, mental energy is entirely beneficent, enhancing the creativity of the artist, soothing the insomniac to sleep while rousing the lethargic, harmonizing the disturbed pathways in the brain which have caused speech and learning defects, uplifting the depressive, and in some instances opening the autistic child to human connection.

Involving as it does a rehabilitation of the ear, Sound Therapy is a process requiring a certain length of time. The effect of the cassette will not be immediate. On an average, 100 to 200 hours of listening are necessary before there is a noticeable change in the energy level and sense of well being. But once the middle ear has been tuned to high frequency response the brain will respond swiftly to the recharge. If you happen to have gone out without your Walkman and arrive home tired, ten minutes' relaxation with the music will be like hours of sleep. Eventually, with regular recharging, you will forget what tiredness was like.

It sounds like magic and it is, magic being simply natural law not previously understood. Tomatis's work is thoroughly scientific; his discoveries have been tested and confirmed by the Sorbonne University in Paris, and given the name The Tomatis Effect. As a result he has been made a member of the French Academy of Medicine and the Academy of Science.

Perhaps the greatest bounty of the Tomatis Effect is its gift of time. Once the opening of the auditory system has occurred, sleep can safely be reduced by two, three or four hours a night, with the waking time becoming more vital and useful. Energy never flags, yet peace and relaxation permeate the hours. This is our own natural energy which has been blocked and is now restored.

Everyone is restricted to some extent by blockages arising from distortions of hearing. During early years, in order not to hear certain unpleasant sounds, a child may deafen himself in the area of high frequencies, cut off his auditory diaphragm and withdraw from communication by involuntarily choosing longer brain circuits. He then loses much of his potential, particularly the ability to listen to language; in extreme cases he may develop dyslexia or other disorders which baffle diagnosis. Tomatis, who discovered for us the strict relationship that exists between our mental attitude and our listening, has successfully treated more than 12,000 subjects for dyslexia by transforming the receptivity of the ear. He found that if there is a failure of hearing at a certain low point of frequency, all the areas above that frequency will be blocked. But when the ear is re-educated and the barrier is lifted, below for instance 1,000 Hz, all the other areas wake up very quickly and the subject is able to benefit from the store of vitality which has been dormant.

We have to distinguish between charging sounds, those rich in high harmonics, and the low, or discharging sounds. In the region of 3,000 to 20,000 Hz, sound mainly serves the function of producing cortical arousal, whereas low frequencies tend to exhaust the system; they can actually be dangerous, as they demand of the body a greater discharge of energy than the cortex receives in stimulation. The sound of the tom-tom, for example, is intended specifically to make the body move and to send the listeners into a secondary state, a sort of hypnosis, which puts them at the mercy of more powerful minds, such as the witch doctor's. High sounds, on the other hand, lead the subject to consciousness and self actualization.

The implication at the psycho-dynamic level is that depressive persons tend to direct their hearing more intensely toward low frequencies; and, as the voice is directly related to the ear, often speak in a low monotone. The ear has lost its ability to be used as an antenna for the life force. In contrast, the person whose ear has been trained to high frequencies begins tuning into these re-charging sounds in the surrounding air, drawing upon an unending source of energy and upliftment. Among all professions, the people with the greatest longevity are or-chestral conductors, who spend the greater part of their waking hours in direct exposure to classical music, which is the kind of music that contains the greatest preponderance of frequencies.

Tomatis says: "What the youth of today is looking for is the stimulation of their brain. The trouble is that they are taken up not with charging sounds but with dis-charging sounds. In the music they play there are no high harmonics. The more they play, the more tired they feel, and the more they are obliged to increase the intensity. That music discharges you; it compels the organism into mechanical movement. Such involvement taxes the mus-culature without recharging the organism."

It is impossible to be in good health when brain sys-tems are not in proper working order, yet the very idea of the brain makes people nervous. "So little is known about the brain," we are told, and the implications are ominous. All this mystery makes the brain seem as scarey as a haunted house; we're afraid to even look in the win-dow, let alone stir things up.

"Recharge the brain?" said one man in alarm. "What happens when the brain can't be recharged any more?"

Well, the time comes for every brain when it can't be recharged any more. It's called death. Until then our brains are continually being charged or discharged by the sounds around us, and we'd be wise to determine what those sounds are going to be, while we still have the brain to do it with. Unless it is kept toned up, the brain merely deteriorates with the advance of years, and there lies the root problem of old age. The real heartbreak for the aged is feeling themselves a burden to others. But you can bet that all branches of the family would be fighting over who was going to have Grandma or Grandpa if these were sparkling companions, full of fresh ideas and wit and the health that is controlled by the master computer of the body. This stage of life awaits us all. Instead of (or along with) the savings in the bank to allow independence when we become a drag, it would be worth our while to accumulate the more fundamental currency of life energy which flows in to us through the brain.

We needn't fear using that energy up like our oil resources. Nowhere is it written: "This much and no more you may have." This is the energy of the cosmos, continually passing through us — or trying to. More often it can't break in and has to surge round us like water round an obstacle in the river. It is all available, if we'll just let it in. Yoga exercises teach us how to bring it into our muscles. Toning the cortex is no different from toning the muscles.

Such toning, with its effect upon the frontal lobes which regulate attention and concentration, makes the therapy particularly valuable for students. Words and ideas are more readily absorbed and retained, and also the power of creativity is heightened. The increase in cortical energy permits the person's thoughts to be expressed more easily, in various creative forms. Through the action upon the basilar membrane, rich in sensory fibres, general perception is improved and the body image harmonized.

It should be emphasized that the electronic technique is in no way designed to condition the subject artificially. It is not intended to conform the ears and the brain, but merely to assist in the full opening of auditory perceptions, so that persons who are traumatized, frustrated or restricted by incidents in their history, may regain the positive freedom of their nature. The maladjustments which have caused a partial closing of the ear tend toward a partial closing of the personality to other people and to the world in general. The therapy has broad psychological applications and fortifies the principles of psychoanalysis, while streamlining the process. Both have the same goal, to obtain the greatest possible maturing of the person. While it takes a great deal of time to be freed of complexes through psychoanalysis, Sound Therapy arrives at the same result by a more direct route, bringing about the maturation of the individual by working directly on the brain structures.

Dr. Sarkissof, a psychoanalyst, speaking at the International Congress of the SECRAP in 1972, describes certain patients whom he had agreed to analyze, rather reluctantly, not holding a great deal of hope for their cure. He states: "The results of these analyses confirmed my doubts as to the possibility of completely curing these patients. The more time passed the more I doubted that I could succeed in obtaining anything more than an improvement of their condition . . . . I decided to let them undergo treatment with the Tomatis apparatus. Not only did they accept willingly, but they accepted with gratitude and high hopes, and I realized, although they had not spoken of it, that all of them were fully aware that treatment by psychoanalysis alone could not completely cure them. The material they offered at the sessions then changed radically. In each of them the Tomatis apparatus brought to light fantasies of a return to the mother's breast and to birth, and the analysis of these fantasies was accompanied by a clearly visible transformation of their entire personality. All these patients shared a core of unconscious autism: their emotional contacts were without warmth and life, their analyses went round in circles without uncovering any particular cause of resistance, which meant a basic difficulty in communication. Sound Therapy rapidly reduced this core of autism. In the space of a few months, the autism gave way to a joyful, outgoing self-awareness, and their co-operation in the analysis became fruitful. My personal reservations regarding these patients gave way to great optimism as to their ability to get well completely. One of the patients expressed his astonishment at noting that he had suddenly become capable of making great progress, readily and without anxiety, while he remembered that before the treatment, the efforts demanded of him in psychoanalysis seemed immense and completely out of proportion to the slight progress he made. He considered the Tomatis treatment a very valuable short cut, which made him feel that he was making a game of his difficulties.''

Dr. Sarkissof explains that our destiny is recorded somewhere inside us as if on a magnetic tape which preserves the memory of what we experience. This store, in turn, plays a determining role in our process of becoming. None of our actions is indifferent but each affects the future, as we constantly recreate ourselves. A magnetic tape is not erased automatically. A special device is required. Thus it is very difficult to erase from our mind the tapes of our past which are recorded in our subconscious. "We have two methods for bringing this about," continues Dr. Sarkissof. "One consists of bringing it onto the conscious level; that is into the present. This is the method of psychoanalysis. It is often very lengthy and demands much courage and perseverance. The Tomatis apparatus brings us another method. It succeeds in erasing the 'tape' without bringing it into the conscious mind. It can eliminate for the patient the suffering of reliving his neurosis. During the treatment he continues to unwind the tape of his life without difficulty. The traumatic experiences of his past are erased from his subconscious directly, for the Tomatis treatment has the advantage of reaching the deepest layers of the subconscious, liberating him from fixations and eliminating the obstacles to normal functioning. The personality is then free to develop unhindered and recover the subconscious energy which was blocked."

The same applies for the mildly neurotic and for the reasonably healthy, like the rest of us. We do the listening for simple brain recharge, yet as our control centres are harmonized, things sort themselves out at deep levels without us ever having to know what they are — or admit they were there. The complex is made simple — an unbelievable occurrence in our desperate and complicated time.

Audio-Psycho-Phonology is a cybernetic system of

appalling complexity, and the literature is enough to stagger the mind. Yet when it comes to the practice the complexities don't matter. It's like electricity: you don't have to understand the principle behind it in order to light your room; all you have to know is how to put in a light bulb and flick a switch. To reap the benefits of Sound Therapy you only have to slide in a cassette and press Start. And the expenditure in time is absolutely nothing. With the Walkman's convenience and portability you can do the complete listening program while continuing all your usual activities — with a few exceptions like tennis and sex.

This isn't to say that listening to the cassettes will cure everything, or that it will do the same thing as the original therapy. Serious problems will require the skills of a trained therapist. The Tomatis equipment conveys a higher frequency than the Walkman, and the Tomatis-trained therapists have other techniques to go with it. The self-conducted system has two main advantages. It makes this great discovery available in some measure to the many instead of the few. And the effects, while they take longer to achieve, can be maintained, in that the person can keep up the listening for months, years, or for life, as most satisfied subjects are resolved to do.

Another consideration is the cost. The price of tapes and a Sony Walkman is a fraction of what people pay for most therapies. And the will power required is minimal compared to analysis or even meditation. In fact Sound Therapy is the perfect therapy for the weak willed.

Still, there must be a sputter of life in the resolve to undertake the daily listening and to accept that the sound is not exactly the same thing as having the best seat at a concert. Some people don't like the high pitched sound of filtered music, though others find it very pleasant. It may be that tolerance is directly related to the desire for self-betterment. Certainly, those who unconsciously desire to hang on to their deafness or sleeplessness or perpetual tiredness are going to object to the sound. In contrast are those self-improvers who become positively addicted to it and lose all interest in 'normal' music. Said one, "I start listening to my regular tapes and soon realize they're not doing anything for me. It's like drinking a highball when you forgot to put in the liquor."

Not that the Tomatis effect bears any relation to the liquor effect. The difference between the alcohol high and this one is that the Sound Therapy lift is healthy and it stays with you. It is a boost onto a higher level in the domain of our vast, unrealized potential. Drink fuzzes the mind, while the sound clarifies it to a high sheen. One person has described the sensation as "like having a new head." Another feels as though her mind had been put through a shower. As the headphones are lifted off after a half hour or so, there is a glowing feeling between the ears, a sense of radiant energy, not the revved-up energy of the chemical high, but a calm and peaceful aliveness, as in those moments when we are very happy, having just had good news, or simply being tuned to the joy of life.

Sound therapists have known that their treatment of various disorders brings wonderful "side effects" in the form of energy and well-being. For the healthy person these constitute a main effect. But healthy persons are not in the habit of seeking treatment to maintain their good condition and raise it to sparkling — though they do it regularly for their cars.

Who would think of going to a sound therapist and saying: "I don't need the treatment, but I'd like the side effects please"? For that matter, who in Canada would think of going to a sound therapist? They can be counted on the fingers of one hand and they're promoted as little as Canadian writers.

But this Canadian writer stumbled over one like a treasure in the dark, and so is obeying the universal rule of supply, which dictates: **Pass it on.**

Chapter Two

Plugged into the Cosmos

Looking back, it doesn't seem strange that I should have been one of the first people in the country to find my way to a sound therapist's door, as most of my life has been lived off the beaten track. For example, you can read about my experiment in allowing my children to educate themselves at home (as distinct from 'educating' them at home) if you care to see my book, **And the Children Played,** reprinted by Tundra Books, Montreal, spring, '84.

One of these children, Melanie, having graduated from college (her first experience of school) was continuing her self-education and spending the year 1977 in Paris to perfect her French. There, by chance as they call it, she met a French-Canadian doctor who was studying Sound Therapy with Dr. Tomatis. Melanie spoke to him about her mother's hearing problem, a matter of great inconvenience to the family, though they were always very nice about it.

My problem was this: I couldn't carry on a conversation if there were other people talking in the room. If I had to talk against the voice background, or listen to someone speaking to me, the cross vibrations of sound simply broke me up. At home I was constantly calling for silence and then trying to get a single conversation going while everybody else held their tongues. It was socially debilitating, to say the least, and it was getting worse. At a publisher's party for one of my books I had to sneak out after a few minutes and go home. Luckily there was lots to drink and I never did hear that anybody noticed.

I had mentioned this malady to a number of people who told me they had it too. So of course the Canadian doctor recognized it at once from the description. He told my daughter that it could be cured with Sound Therapy. She asked him what Sound Therapy was, and considering the explanation that found its way back to me, it's a good thing I go on faith.

Accordingly, when he returned to Montreal to set up practice the following spring, I was right there. We had a nice talk, (no one else was speaking in the room) and a few days later my treatment commenced.

All was mystery from the word go, and the word was not Go, it was Beep. Connected by headphones to an unearthly looking machine, on which the therapist produced high-pitched sounds by twirling a handle, I had to state when I heard what, and where. During all this he was drawing a graph with coloured pencils. I felt strangely elated by these high tones and attributed it to the total yogic concentration necessary to decide whether they came from right, left or centre. I was also asked whether a sequence of sounds was getting higher or lower. They were all sky high and sometimes I just didn't know. I gave answers, then took them back. It was like sitting for an examination that I didn't want to fail.

The headphones were changed for another pair that didn't go on my ears at all. They fitted over the mastoid bone and the bone at my temple. I was amazed to find that I could hear through my bones as well as through my ears. It was the first I knew of the fact that we hear with our whole body. This was downtown Montreal and the traffic sounds outside were like an artillery attack. They had devastated me previously and were now made harmless by these eloquent little electronic bleeps. I could hardly believe my ears — or my ears could scarcely believe the soothing yet stimulating sound that promised an end to abuse.

When the listening test was completed, the therapist was able to view the precise nature of my trouble. He saw another one that I hadn't thought to mention . . . for how could it relate to sound? It was my complete help-lessness at all things technical. Like a clairvoyant he read this from the graph. It was absolutely true. I could bare-ly change a light bulb, couldn't possibly replace a fuse, and always had to get some small child to put in my type-writer ribbon. On the day the stereo system was delivered and the kids were showing me how to use it, I am quoted as saying: "Oh, I have to press Stop? I'll never be able to work that." The family was still laughing. (But the last laugh would be mine.)

Next, the therapy was explained to me — in simple words, with respect to my deficiencies in the technical field. As it is quite impossible to really put across the principles of Sound Therapy in simple words, I again had to take it on faith. It seemed that a specific listening program would be designed for me. This would consist largely of the music of Mozart, and I would sit and listen to it for three hours every week-day during the next six weeks.

"That's all?" I asked. "There's nothing more to it?"

"Yes. Bring some sewing or embroidery to work on. It's better to absorb the sound subconsciously, with the attention fixed on something else."

It turned out that women patients did needlework and men did jigsaw puzzles. I was gladder than ever to be a female.

Game for anything, I settled into the routine, driving the sixty miles from my farm at St. Agnes de Dundee and sitting for three hours daily, comfortably settled in an armchair in a little room, with my headphones, my sewing and my thermos of tea. The music was recognizably Mozart, though Mozart would have had a fit. The violin concertos, symphonies and chamber pieces all started out normally, except for occasional soft hissing sounds. Then, imperceptibly, the lower sounds began giving way to the strings. After a time even the strings were clinging to the rafters. It was strange, eerie, and perversely pleasing. Yet I wondered. It just didn't seem possible that sitting here listening to squeaky music for three hours was going to relieve me of anything but thirty-six dollars. (By now the fee is considerably higher, all low prices having been filtered out everywhere.)

The equipment from which all this originated was

stacked in the next room and operated by an assistant. It looked pretty spooky with its blinking lights and turning reels, and I always hurried past it, while noting that wires snaked under several doors to other patients in their comfy little dens. It was good to know that others were willing to take a chance, though when I stopped to think of it, I never saw them. I pondered about what their personalized listening programs might be like while I imbibed the one specifically designed to sort out the crossed wires in my head — or whatever it was that so inhibited the social life I didn't much want. I was really doing this from a fear that my hearing quirk might lead to deafness. I had seen my mother gradually lose her hearing and become isolated from human company and, almost worse, from music. Nietzche said it when he said: "Without music life would be a mistake."

I stuck this out week after week, trying lamely to explain at home the purpose of the daily trek. They surmised that Sound Therapy was some kind of faith healing. If that's what it was it wouldn't work, because I was starting to lose faith. Also, there was no sign of healing. I observed my reactions with mounting anxiety, like a hypochondriac taking her own pulse every few minutes. I was neither better nor worse. I began to resent the time that was going into this. And the car was eating up a lot of gas.

The fourth week offered a little variety in the form of a vocalizing technique. A microphone was set up on the table in my little room and a new tape relayed through the headphones. A female voice gave instructions, then spoke sibilant words at high frequency, leaving a gap between each. In the gap I was to repeat the word into the microphone. As I did this, my own voice, also filtered to very high pitch, came back into my ears. Due to past experience as a radio actress I felt quite at home with the mike, though I never expected to be presented with a script like this.

Next, a monk with a beautiful voice came on singing phrases of Gregorian chant, with cathedral echo backup. He too waited for my repetition, and I was glad he couldn't hear it, for I never could carry a tune.

It was all terribly wearing. A deep exhaustion settled over me. My therapist had warned that I might get a little tired: it would mean that the therapy was working, the effect beginning to be felt in the muscle of the middle ear, the brain patterns rearranging themselves. He explained it again. I couldn't follow any of it. I hadn't the strength. The exhaustion that had seeped into me could only be compared with the depleted feeling that follows childbirth — or finishing a novel. Arriving home at night after the sixty-mile drive, I could hardly drag myself out of the car. I detested driving anyway; cars were technical and I hated them.

And then — how did it begin? I first noticed it at the wheel, while stopped in the rush-hour traffic. It was a kind of gentle vibration in my head, a sense of something about to take off. I began singing, using the humming technique I had learned in my sessions. I sang my way out of Montreal and hummed as I spun along the highway. When I got home I noted with surprise that I was not tired. Far from it. I stayed up late doing things around the house, and rose early the next morning, deeply rested and refreshed. The effect was subtle — not a high-powered charge but a sure, calm sense of energy; it was energy formerly untapped, now available, ready to be drawn upon as needed. The feeling of well-being increased day by day, peaking at moments — usually in the evening when I would ordinarily be flaked out — and sending a dynamism sparking along my veins as though I were electrically connected. I told my therapist: "I feel as though I've been plugged into the cosmos."

He only smiled. He knew about this. For one thing he had taken the therapy himself in France as part of his training. His serenity was one of the characteristic results. Yet I saw him excited too — on the day when he opened the door of another listening room and pointed to a child wearing headphones and stretched out on a sofa. "That child," he told me softly, "was so hyper that his parents were going to have to institutionalize him. Now he lies still for three hours every day listening to Mozart." Later the boy's mother came for treatment also, and the family found harmony.

Within a week I was going around in a perpetual state of exultation. Before my therapy began I'd been working on a novel. It had struck a roadblock and stopped. Suddenly the words began flowing again. I sat scribbling all through my sessions and was still working at home at midnight, though ordinarily I wasn't able to write beyond noon. (That book was **The Selena Tree,** published by McClelland and Stewart, now in New Canadian Library paperback edition. You might note the dedication.)

I seemed to feel no need for sleep. When I went to bed it was not because I was tired, but because the next day had rolled around and I thought I ought to. For years I had had difficulty sleeping and had made a huge point of going to bed at nine, to read for an hour and toss around for another two, in order to be asleep by midnight and get the eight hours I needed for a good morning's work. This meant I had no evenings and neither did the others in the house, who had to tiptoe around and keep their talk to a whisper. Now I was seeing them off to bed while I charged around the house, typing, cooking, cleaning, catching up on correspondence and all those things which drag at the mind. When I lay down to sleep — miraculously, I slept.

On an afternoon in my sixth and final week, as I sat listening in my little room, the therapist came strolling in. I tensed up, in mortal fear that he was going to say something. Not only did I have to keep silent when there were voices in the background, but also when music was playing.

He began to speak. I went into my act, waving my hands frantically and objecting: "I've got the music on! I can't talk when there's music on, I never could!"

He smiled and said calmly: "You can now."

I stopped short and listened to him. I ventured to answer. We chatted about many things and the music played on, and he was right: I had been cured.

I went out into the stores and talked to salespeople, with the babble of voices all around me. No problem. I couldn't believe it. Neither could my family when I got home that night. I walked into the house and all talk stopped, as usual. "Go right on," I said airily. "Doesn't bother me a bit."

Now I became intensely curious as to what had happened. I had asked several times: "What does the sound do exactly?" and could never understand the answer. It couldn't be told in a few sentences. (One would have to write a book!) It had to do with recharging the cortex of the brain and was accompanied by some sort of theory about a return to the womb and a rebirth through sound. This clarified the picture for me as much as seeing it through water.

"It works," the therapist said. "That's what counts."

It was true. From that day to this I have never been troubled by crosscurrents of voices — though my daughters were disappointed about the paper bags. You see, along with everything else, my hearing has always been very acute, and there was something about the resonating crackle of paper bags being folded that struck my eardrums like spears. On shopping day, therefore, as we unpacked the groceries, I was always warning: "Don't fold the bags till I'm out," and finally left the kitchen awash in open, empty paper bags.

So the girls had hoped my therapy would take care of this too. But the effect of the sound is to open the hearing — so it was worse with the bags. Nothing's perfect.

As the day approached when my listening sessions were to end, I began to feel bereft. What if it all wore off? I asked my therapist — I begged him: "Isn't there some way I could listen to this kind of music at home?"

He assured me there wasn't. "You would have to buy all this." He waved at the equipment. "It cost twenty thousand dollars."

If I'd had the twenty thousand, I'd have spent it on that in a minute.

"Even then," he went on, "you wouldn't know how to use it."

That was certainly true. And given the state of technological development at that time, he was right that there was no way. He wasn't lying to me. He just didn't know he was talking to someone at whom the eye of fate had just winked.

After the final session he gave me the listening test again, and was able to show me on the graph the changes that had taken place. I didn't have to see the graph. A graph is only two dimensional lines. I knew in all the complex dimensions of myself the transformation that had occurred. I hugged him wordlessly and left. I felt strangely alone, unconnected from the equipment.

As weeks passed, I slowly became unconnected from the cosmos too. The radiant energy flickered and faded. At the end of the day I was tired like anybody else. Sleep eluded me again, although there was no sign of the malady which had driven me to Sound Therapy. The cure was effective, but I mourned the loss of the side effects. For that I would have traded the cure in a twinkling.

I tried to cheer myself by going to some parties, now being normal, audiometrically speaking. Though I could stand the sound of voices, I remembered that I couldn't stand parties. I walked the fields, humming desperately. The humming technique I'd been taught was the one scrap of self help possible. I hummed until the birds all fled from that part of Quebec. It helped a little, but without the high frequencies to back it up I was humming in the dark.

Writer's block struck again, and I was devastated. But there was something I could do for this. I developed a pattern: whenever I was seriously stuck I would phone Montreal and make an appointment for one Sound Therapy session. The three hours of listening never failed to get my inspiration flowing.

Evidently I was tied for life to the Montreal area, or maybe Toronto, where I understood there was one other sound therapist practising.

Life is cruel, and circumstances conspired to move me two years later to the Saskatchewan prairie. Settled in a tiny, charming old farmhouse in the Minichinas Hills, I knew it was the perfect place for me to live and write. Yet the real place of writing was in my head, and I would cheerfully have camped at the intersection of Peel and Ste. Catherine Streets if I could have had again the limitless vitality, the calm and drugless high that brought my inspiration to me like Joan's angel voices on the wind.

Two years passed, and ever my mind strained eastward. Running like an underground river through my thoughts were plans and schemes for getting more Sound Therapy. I was on the point more than once of applying as Writer-in-Residence at Montreal's Concordia University, a mad idea as I scarcely take up residence even in my own house but have to be always in the fresh air, doing my writing under the sky.

Some people have a vivid, lifelong, shining memory of the moment when they were proposed to; or informed that they had won the Irish sweepstake; or received the inspiration for a great invention. I will carry a vivid, lifelong shining memory of the moment, one evening in my prairie farmhouse, when my dinner guest, Russ Powell, idly said:

"Oh, you know St. Peter's Abbey up at Muenster?"

I didn't know it. I just knew Muenster on the map.

"I have a relative by marriage there," he continued, "a monk named Father Lawrence —"

I stifled a yawn.

"— and he's working with the same therapy you took in Montreal."

"*What?*" I sprang up, toppling my chair. Russ looked a little alarmed. "Sound Therapy?"

"Yes," he said. "I went up last week and he demonstrated the listening test for me. They're using the therapy with the pre-vocation students at St. Peter's College there."

Muenster? *Muenster?* Could it be possible?

Russ described the listening test and the electronic set-up. There was no doubt: it was the same. On the thousands of miles of prairie, I had landed blind, forty-eight miles from the kingdom.

Next morning at the crack of dawn I phoned St. Peter's, and of course found people up. Father Lawrence listened to my incoherent plea, and invited me to supper at the Abbey. There, in impeccably kept grounds and buildings, I found an alive brotherhood of educators, farmers and innovators. Father Lawrence DeMong was a warm, dynamic person, a practical visionary who had introduced Sound Therapy into the school more than two years before. It was already here, I realized, when I was drawn across the country by . . . what? That force which goes by many names.

He said: "I believe that Religious Houses like ours should be crossing new frontiers. Here's a new frontier which is really exciting but is not being crossed very rapidly. That's why we as an Abbey took this initiative."

Initiative didn't stop there. At supper I met Brother Oswald, who was into health foods and brought all his own makings to meals — raw vegetables, sunflower seeds, tofu, brown bread, herbal tea. He also practised Iridology and treated his brethren with a few other way-out healing techniques. They themselves didn't bother with the Sound Therapy, however. The listening took too much time and they were busy men.

After the meal Father Lawrence escorted me to the College wing where the listening lab was located. And there it was — the self-same array of intricate machines, all twenty thousand dollars worth. Twice: for there were two listening rooms side by side, each with its Electronic Ear and reel-to-reels and all the supporting gadgets.

My head still hadn't caught up with my feet, which had transported me as in a dream to this monastery in the middle of nowhere, which I found equipped with the very latest in electronic wizardry, leading the way toward new heights in education, healing and personal development. I couldn't quite grasp what this bearded priest in his blue jeans and sneakers was telling me. I *thought* he said I could come and listen just as much as I wanted to. Was it possible that he could give up all that time for my treatment? And I wondered if I could afford it. I inquired about the fee. He waved my question away with a smile.

"I'll give you a key to the listening room," he said. "You can come and listen any hour of the day or night."

Did that mean he intended to turn up at those times to operate the machinery?

"The listening rooms are in use during school hours, but come as early as you'd like in the mornings . . . or you may prefer the evening. Stay all night if you want." He gestured to the sofas in the room. "Would you like to start immediately?"

"But what about my listening program?" I ventured to ask. Surely he had to work that out first.

"There are the tapes." He indicated a shelf lined with reel boxes. "They're all labelled. The 8,000 hertz gives the quickest recharge, but you can vary them for interest. Just help yourself."

I broke in politely. "Who's going to work the equipment, Father?"

"You are."

Me?

"I'll teach you right now," he said briskly. "I have a few minutes before prayers." With an eye on his wrist-watch, he flicked on the machines, and taking it for granted that I could understand plain English, said: "You adjust the intensity with this Gate — the Recorder lever has the same effect so you can use a combination of the two to throw the light from red to green, and the oftener you switch them the better. These dials control lateralization; you might want your right ear dominance to start at five and ten and work up to one and ten. Don't rush it. This is Volume, this is Power, be sure to turn it off when you leave."

"Do I have to press Stop?" I asked.

"No, it stops automatically."

That was something anyway.

He selected one of the tapes at random and threaded it swiftly and deftly onto the reel. I think he had the impression he was showing me how. In the end I learned the whole business the way I learned to drive: got going with the thing and worked it out.

But I asked him now: "How will I know which tape to play first?"

"The sequence makes no difference at all. I'll get your key now." He started for the door.

"But — but," I stammered, "What if I overdo it?"

"You can't overdo it. There's no way this sound can harm you. The more listening you do, the better. Some have listened for eight hours a day and it did them nothing but good." He went bounding off down the hall.

I looked at the Electronic Ear and it blinked its lights at me. Was this man actually going to leave us alone together?

Father hurried back in and handed me the key. "Sorry to run off. Happy listening!" he said, and rushed off to pray. I stood there with the key in my hand, the perfect symbol. It was the key to the kingdom.

But there was work ahead. First I sat down to listen to the tape that was already running on the reel. I was curious to hear what music they played here. I put on the headphones and to my amazement recognized the identical recording that had formed part of my therapy in Montreal. I wondered if the others were the same, though my curiosity was not satisfied quickly. It took me hours to get through another couple of half hour tapes. Yet I made progress. For instance, after a reel had fallen off the deck a few times and rolled across the floor with me crawling after it, I figured out the purpose of the little knob that holds it on.

And each tape I heard was a dupicate of those which I had thought designed for my particular hearing problem. In Montreal I had had the clear impression that the music and the order of the music were part of a personalized program. Here, as the guest of St. Peter's, I was invited to help myself. There hadn't even been any talk of a listening test — though they had the testing device, because there it was over in the corner.

I had enough to figure out for one night, so I let that one go.

By the time I turned everything off and locked the door the Abbey was silent and dark, with low lights in the corridors to guide me out. The outer doors were unlocked and unattended, with only the ancient trees standing guard. The moon spread its light over the stately grounds and gardens, and as I walked to my car I thought of what they said, people like these, about the answer to prayer — even if they had to run for it, as a result of setting someone on the path.

I rose before five the next morning in order to get to the Abbey by six o'clock. That way I could have three hours' listening before school started. I couldn't be sure it was really true until I fitted the key in the lock and found that it turned, admitting me to the room that was to become my second home. It was a large room, full of light, with a reclining chair and several couches. Tall win-

dows gave a view of prairie sky, and below, the vast and
perfect lawns. This time I omitted the sewing. I brought
the tea and my writing pad. I brought my hopes. . . and
they promised to be fulfilled. By nine o'clock the subtle
dynamo was again whirring in my brain, though it would
take a week to return to its former strength. I thought of
the way people kiss the earth when they return to their
native land after exile. I could have kissed the hardwood
floor.

Better not, for the students were traipsing in, four
or five big lads, casting curious looks at me in my headphones. Father Lawrence had said I might stay and share
the facilities with them whenever I wished, as there were
plenty of headphones, with small Volume/Balance boxes
on the floor to plug them into. At a later date he told
me it did the kids good to see that someone would come
in here and listen to this stuff of her own free will. For
them it was compulsory, of course, since this was school.
Compulsory or voluntary, it worked the same. I
watched, marvelling, as they collected their headphones
from the shelves and plugged them in and stretched out
on the couches. If school had been like this for me, what
might I not have amounted to by now?

I offered to let them change the tape I was playing if
they wanted another. They said that was okay, it didn't
matter, and plunked on their headphones and went to
sleep.

It was clicking into place for me. It really didn't make
any difference which tape you listened to, or what order
you played them in. I had discovered that this entire set
of tapes was identical to the ones I'd heard in Montreal,

and was to find out that indeed the master tapes were made by Dr. Tomatis in Paris and purchased by the therapists, who then made their own copies. The therapeutic value was not in the assortment or the sequence, but in the filtering and Electronic Ear effect. The high frequency was imprinted on every tape and played to the patient through the Electronic Ear. You could have taken any one of them and benefitted to the full by playing it often enough. The only trouble was you'd tire of it, and that was the reason for the variety of music.

There was also a variation in the degree of filtering. One half hour tape began at normal and was gradually filtered up to 8,000 Hz. The next to be played was 8,000 Hz from start to finish. A third began at 8,000 and slowly descended to normal. That was the listening program. There was no deception in calling it that; it's just that the program was the same here as it had been in Montreal and came down to the fact that all you have to do is play the music. After a certain length of time the brain becomes harmonized and energized. It then begins giving the right signals to the rest of the system, and ease replaces dis-ease.

Father Lawrence acknowledged that that's what it boiled down to. Yet he claimed it was useful to give the students the listening test; it provided an accurate diagnosis, and the students' progress could then be checked.

A case in point: before the school term ended I was invited to address the English class. I read from one of my plays, and afterwards a girl came up to me and expressed her appreciation. She was quite eloquent. When she had moved on, Sister Miriam Spenrath, her English teacher, said to me: "One year ago that girl had such a speech defect that you could hardly understand her. She's been on the Sound Therapy program, listening an hour a day for one year. Her latest listening test showed an eighty percent improvement."

I hadn't noticed any flaw in the girl's speech at all. I wondered why they needed a machine to measure her improvement and couldn't just measure it by the girl. But that's science for you.

At the same time I could understand why the therapy had to be framed into a structure for treating the public. It has been established that the average time required for the effect is 100 to 200 hours. Therefore my initial six weeks, at fifteen hours a week, was pretty close and fulfilled its claim by healing my intolerance to cross-vibrations of sound. If the six weeks was not long enough to lock in the accompanying gift of radiant energy, well, that was never presented as a feature of the therapy. It was simply a bonus which came along for a time, and which I wanted to grasp and hang onto for life.

Now the question arose — was it possible to make permanent connection with that great reservoir of energy, to which we ordinarily have such a clogged pipeline? As far as I could discover, no one had ever listened long enough to find out. Unless you were really suffering, the therapy was too great a sacrifice in time. No one wanted to sit hour after hour, helplessly plugged in, while life with its demands clamoured outside the door. Even Father Lawrence who directed the program said he sat down in the lab and listened only when desperately tired or preparing for some test of endurance.

Well, if that was the only problem, I was going to make myself a test case. I settled into a routine which I was determined to stick to for as long as it took. Rising at four a.m. every day, I left the house at five, drove into the Abbey grounds at six, and listened for three hours alone with my writing. I got a lot of work done and started to really enjoy the technical business of manipulating the tapes and reels. Monitoring the Electronic Ear myself gave a sense of direct contact, of being in touch, like running my own life instead of having it controlled from the next room. I was getting the hang of this fabulous equipment, and was still amazed that anyone would leave me alone with it. There were dozens of dials and levers that had to do with recording; these I eyed with fear and was careful not to touch.

I put on the tape with the sibilant sounds and had a go at the microphone; also the Gregorian chant. The voice recharge in combination with the ear was considered extremely valuable, and I could feel the effect immediately. But the mike was a hassle, and I decided to do my singing on the prairie, where I walked miles every day anyway. I hit on the idea of plugging my ears with cotton for return resonance and felt a good effect from it. The reason the humming worked for me, where it hadn't on my farm walks in Quebec, was that now I had the boost of the daily high frequencies. I would also find with time that I could sing in tune, as I never could before.

After about a week I was back to the energy level of the therapy days in Montreal. Because of that groundwork, the whole process was speeded up this time. Around the middle of the week I again passed through the sluggish sea of tiredness, but left it behind after a day or two. Despite the four a.m. rising I rode high on energy all day and once more was able to cut out the hour's rest I'd always needed after lunch. Time was very precious to me and I had always resented the time given for sleep — that daytime hour especially. I did start to fade out after supper and began to wish I lived next door to the Abbey, for I knew that half an hour's listening would set me up again for the evening.

The two hours a day I had to spend on the road were quite a loss, but I tried not to worry about that. The gains were worth it. I whiled away the journey listening to symphonies on my Sony Walkman, a new acquisition which I treasured above all things. Father Lawrence spotted it one day and was immediately interested. This was before everybody and his brother had one, and the marvel of it was still new. Actually, he was interested in getting one for his brother, who had a birthday coming up. Always conscious of frequencies, he asked me what the frequency response was. As if I would know! I looked it up in the booklet that night, and next morning I told him. It was 16,000 hertz.

"Sixteen thousand!" he exclaimed. "Why, it's high enough for you to do your therapy on the Walkman."
We were standing at dead centre of the main lobby, in a pool of sunlight which came pouring down from a high window. He was wearing his black robes and beyond him the sun caught the switchboard, the girl dressed in pink behind the glass, sparkling like a fish in tropical waters. The details are etched on my memory, because

it was another of those moments that cast their aura over the whole of life.

"Buy some metal cassettes," he went on briskly. "Half a dozen should do. Bring them with you tomorrow. I'll set up a cassette deck in the lab and take the day off and we'll record the whole program for you." He said that while their equipment ran to 20,000 hertz, it took a very sensitive ear to hear 16,000. And he knew that the cheap imitations of the Walkman didn't approach that level. It would seem that with a little extra listening to the cassettes, the Sony should yield the full therapy effect.*

I drove home with my tires one foot off the road. That afternoon I went shopping for metal cassettes. When I discovered the price I hardly flinched. At the cost of the formal Tomatis therapy per hour, I would pay as much to listen for that length of time just *once*.

Next day the listening lab was closed to the students. Some of them listened in the other listening room, while the remainder spent the time cleaning the schoolrooms and seemed to much prefer it. Father Lawrence was expert at recording, bringing into action some more of the mysterious lights and buttons. Completely awed I watched him juggling wires, twirling knobs and dials and monitoring the dance of the arrows. I thought again how far the Church had come. Time was, he'd have been burned at the stake for this.

At the end of the afternoon he placed the six cassettes in my hands and said, "We'll miss you, but now you can do all your listening at home."

---

* It has since been established that 15,000 hertz is sufficient.

So now the prayer was fully answered and there was nothing more to do.

(Oh no?)

It happened that the next day I couldn't do my listening at home, for it was shopping day, the occasion of the week that always filled me with dread. Though a mixture of voices could now be tolerated, I remained atmosphere sensitive and couldn't stand the din of traffic or the psychically crushing environment of supermarkets and shopping malls. My daughter did the driving, which helped; and she lugged everything around and made decisions after my mind was blown. This was not the daughter who had introduced me to Sound Therapy, but my youngest, Felicity, whom I now lived with in a delightful partnership not in the least marred by her total indifference to the discovery which had changed my life. She loved rock (which accounted for us long ago introducing headphones into the house), and thought Tomatis an old fogey who just didn't know real music when he heard it.

Well, if I couldn't listen to my new therapy cassettes at home, at least I could take them with me. I played the music throughout the forty minute drive to Saskatoon, and the half hour finding a place to park, with the volume set low so that we could talk. Then I kept it on, the Walkman tucked in my shoulder bag, as we went around the stores.

Soon an amazing thing became apparent. It was as though I walked on a battlefield with a shield held before me and my head protected by armour. The noise was still there; my mind registered the fact like information of no particular significance. If there were cross-currents of psychic agitation, they found in my immediate atmosphere a wall of harmony that could not be breached.

After an hour or two, when I would normally have been a wreck, I was discovering that shopping could be fun. I wanted to investigate the sales. But we didn't have time, because it was turning into "one of those days." As chance would have it — or was it fateful design? — our ancient Volvo broke down three (3) times in traffic, making us the focus of all eyes as we waited for the mechanic. I drew some particularly strange looks, sitting there under a mantle of tranquility with my headphones on, and being somewhat beyond the age of the average music addict. The spectators would have been even more surprised if they could have heard what I was hearing.

The thought that they might hear it one day did not flower just then, but the seed may have stirred in the serene depths of my mind. It was the next morning as I walked out on the prairie with my Walkman, listening to the sweet high frequencies for the first time beneath the open sky, that the idea sprang up full blown. This gift which had landed in my lap was surely not intended for me alone — or for the few who already knew of it. Presently it was limited to the elect, to those who lived in Toronto or Montreal, and could pay the price — most especially the three hours a day sitting immobilized. Those had to be people in real trouble. But everybody is in a little bit of trouble. Who doesn't need more energy, more time, more peace of mind?

A lot of people already owned a Walkman. Even if they had to buy one . . . I placed it against the alternative, which is to own the original equipment, at 20,000 Hz and

$20,000. That's a dollar a hertz. The Sony Walkman at 16,000 Hz and a price of, let's say, a hundred dollars (some models are less, some more) works out to 1/160th of the cost. Judging by my experience in town the previous day, the lower frequency response didn't make that much difference. And once people had the therapy cassettes, they could also play them on their home tape decks, many at 18,000 to 20,000 Hz.

And who was going to get this going? I looked up at the vast prairie sky and knew I was elected. I stumbled into a gopher hole, which provided perspective and encouraged me to sit down and think about the whole thing.

I would have to research the subject, write about it, talk a lot, and experiment with the cassettes to see if they would work as well as the standard therapy. This meant getting some cassettes in circulation. I couldn't very well copy the Tomatis tapes and hand them out, so would have to produce my own. That meant making master tapes.

That meant finding out how the music was filtered — and doing it. The therapists obtained the music already filtered, and simply ran it through the Electronic Ear directly to the patient. I would have to filter the music and record it in the same process with the Electronic Ear.

Ye gods, I'd have to understand the Electronic Ear!

But why had I been trying so hard to shake my brain awake, if it wasn't to understand more, learn more, do more with my life? If this was a little more than I'd bargained for, maybe I was forgetting the Bargainer at the other end of the deal.

I drove up to St. Peter's that afternoon and explained

why I was back so soon. I wanted to go about introducing Sound Therapy, economy style, mobile and self directed, to a larger public. The monks accepted the idea as logical, practical, and therefore quite likely inspired. I was offered the full use of their facilities, and all the help I needed to go with them. It was a good thing they threw in the second part of the offer. I mentioned that I didn't even know how the music was filtered. They informed me that it was done with two filtering machines, and they already possessed these at the Abbey, for the filtering of mothers' voices. (More about that later.)

"They're a bit complicated," Father Lawrence said cheerfully.

A bit? The moment I came face to face with those filters my heart failed me. The monks gathered round. "You can do it," they said.

There was a sound expert in the Order, a young brother with the patience of Job, and he was assigned to instruct me in the Catechism of Electronics.

And bit by bit the mysterious became knowable, the complex yielded its secrets and stood revealed as simple. Well anyway, possible. I learned how to record the music from records onto reels, filtering the low frequencies out imperceptibly, so that the ear doesn't know what's happening and adjusts painlessly to the high sounds that are ambrosia for the brain. At the same time it was being recorded through the Electronic Ear. But when transferred from reels to cassettes, there were problems of distortion in the high frequencies.

How to solve it? That's what I had to figure out. Everyone was very busy around there, and I couldn't forever be pressing the button to central switchboard — the one I used the most — and calling for Brother William. It was summer; school was out and the listening lab, now converted to recording room, was mine. Along with the original pieces of equipment there were now two cassette decks, a turntable, amplifier, and the two big black frequency equalizers with their special filter adaptations. To this I added a few electric devices of a personal sort: my typewriter, a kettle for my tea, a negative ion generator (we won't get into that right now) and a lamp on a long cord for better scrutiny of the numbered levers in the midnight hours. I'm surprised I didn't blow the whole monastery into eternal darkness. There were so many wires that strangers happening in might have thought they were in a den of snakes. I learned to make my way through them, trailing more wires from my ears, and only occasionally getting so tangled up I resorted to prayer — or words of that nature.

There wasn't much danger of strangers wanting to come in. All that summer, visitors passing the open door stopped and froze. The place looked more as though it belonged to Buck Rogers than to God. But God is showing His scientific streak these days, and if some of it falls on His shadow side, all the more reason to catch what is thrown with the other hand and run with it.

I was experimenting and learning at the same time, working every day and late into the nights. My learning was from the ground up, as I reached for the stars. The combining of filtered music with the Electronic Ear in a single process presented problems which no one had ever encountered before. Anyone with real experience at recording would not have tried. Here was where complete ignorance had the advantage. I didn't know it couldn't work, so stumbled blindly along seeking answers. Not quite blindly: I had tips from the monks as they poked their heads in from time to time to see how I was getting on. Some ventured in further and asked if they might listen; they had always wondered what this Sound Therapy was all about.

An important advisor was Father Andrew, principal of the College. He was knowledgeable about music and familiar with the equipment. Dropping in one day he casually offered a piece of counsel which proved to be crucial — something I wouldn't have hit on in a thousand years.

I made many friends. Brother Oswald, quick to spot another health freak, stopped by in stray moments to talk about healing systems. He knew them all. I learned quite a bit about Iridology. Iridology isn't much known yet in the outer world, so no one had better try telling me that the monastic life means withdrawal from the business of human progress. It seemed to me a truth that you have to step back in order to get a broader and more selective view.

Father Lawrence was always around in the background. As the Abbey's sound therapist he had a few summer patients coming in from outside. He used the equipment in the next room, as I had this one tied up, and conducted the treatment in the same way he had with me: he showed them how to work everything, then left them to it. He still couldn't spare the time to do any listening himself. One of his patients was Sister Anne Honig

from Edmonton; she was spending her vacation at the
Abbey, having chosen it for its Sound Therapy facility.
She was one of the few visitors who wasn't afraid to ask
me what I was doing. We shared midnight tea and she
tried out some of my cassettes. A few of the monks were
testing them for me too, using my Walkman. I often lent
it out for the day and sometimes had trouble finding it
when I wanted to go home. I never travelled without it.

Driving home at night or in the very early mornings,
I listened to the cassettes I'd made that day to check them
out. This was after listening to high frequencies for eight
or ten hours at a stretch. When I saw the sky shimmer-
ing with Northern lights I thought possibly it was coming out of my head. Yet despite this perpetual high, sleep
came to me as to a child. I found it true that as the energy
rises the relaxation deepens, and the expansion is an indication of expanding life.

It started happening that I would walk into the recording room and run into one monk or another, apolo-
gizing to me for using the space, but as everything was
set up and adjusted he thought he'd just turn out a few
cassettes of his own. Father Lawrence had persuaded the
Muenster Elks, a wide awake, forward looking group,
to donate a number of Walkmans, and he had gone out
and bought a hundred metal tapes. He explained to me
that you saved money buying in quantity, though I already knew that argument well.

So at last this marvellous vitalizing sound that he had
brought to the Abbey was accessible to him; he had the
time to listen — because it didn't take any. Parish priest,
educator, therapist, he kept up with it all as he strode

around with his headphones on and his Walkman in the pocket of his robe. It was a boon, another father told me, because he hadn't been sleeping well before he started this, and their early rising applied whether they slept or not.

Brother William, my mentor, was off for a year's study at a seminary in the States, and cassette players were not allowed. He obtained special permission to bring his Sony Walkman and the therapy cassettes, as an aid to study. Sister Anne, whose therapy had been doing so much good she dreaded leaving it, headed back to Edmonton with a Walkman and six-pack of cassettes.

By the end of the summer, half a dozen monks, a handful of nuns and the janitor were walking around St. Peter's with headphones on. Transferred to Ottawa, Father Lawrence made the drive alone at the wheel with a minimum of sleep (a few snoozes), listening to the therapy cassettes all the way.

Word travelled to the sisters at the Ursuline Convent of Bruno not far away. Two of their elderly sisters were suffering from Alzheimer's disease, that dread deterioration of the brain for which there is no cure. Might the Sound Therapy help? They bought four Walkmans and a collection of cassettes. Six weeks later the nursing staff reported that the two sisters with Alzheimer's were "greatly improved — more settled, less hyper and enjoying the music recreationally."

The word from Ottawa was that Father Lawrence wasn't listening much any more, because every time he met a kid with severe problems he gave away his whole set-up.

Early in the fall the decision was made at St. Peter's

College to introduce the Walkman system in the class-rooms so that the students could listen as they worked. More cassettes would have to be made. But the equipment in the recording room was all disassembled. Brother William had gone; Father Lawrence had gone. Many of the monks knew how to handle run-of-the-mill recording, but this meant getting into the really complicated stuff. So guess who was called in to advise?

I'd been so busy through the summer that a certain point had escaped my attention. It was one afternoon as I sat deeply concentrated, monitoring four machines at once, that it hit me. This was the same person who once couldn't get along with a toaster!

What had caused the transformation? It was the sound itself, opening my mind to capacities that had been slumbering, snoring in fact, so deep asleep they would have moved without stirring into the grave.

And what else was sleeping there, and sleeps in everyone? We're told that even geniuses use only ten percent of their brain. Within his own operative ten percent one genius named Tomatis had found a way for us to begin the trek into the limitless potential of the rest.

Oh and by the way, you can fold all the paper bags you want while I'm around, as long as I get my head-phones on first.

Chapter Three

The Tomatis Effect

He was intrigued by work done with unborn birds showing how they recognize the voices of their mothers. This statement captured him: "The eggs of song birds hatched under silent foster mothers produce songless young."

Was it possible that a similar phenomenon might occur in utero between the human mother and child? Hypothesizing that at some time in prenatal life, the foetus might be able to hear the sounds produced by the mother's voice, Dr. Tomatis decided to explore what he thought the intra-uterine world might sound like.

He wrapped a microphone and speaker in a thin rubber membrane and immersed them in water. The speaker was connected to a tape of one of his client's voices. The microphone was connected to another tape recorder, thus registering the sound from the speaker when passed through water. The sound was extraordinary. It reminded him of a deep African night beside the river, contain-

ing unusually high frequencies, mostly above 8,000 Hz
When tested on patients, listening to their mother's voices
recorded through layers of water, the foundation was laid
for new research into foetal life. Since then it has been
proven that the foetus does hear. Its ear is functional from
the fourth month; from that time it hears the mother's
voice and registers all the sounds of her vegetative life.

Early in his experiments, Tomatis had referred to him
a fourteen-year-old autistic child, who had apparently cut
himself off from communication at the age of four. A
filtered recording was made of the mother's voice and
played to the child. The results were dramatic: the boy
turned off the lights in the room, curled up on his
mother's lap in a foetal position and sucked his thumb
throughout the session. Tomatis gradually reduced the
filtering until the voice was like normal air-conducted
sound. As the filtering was reduced the boy began to babble like a ten-month-old child. Thus was born the term
Sonic Birth, the passage from audition in liquidian milieu
to audition in aerial milieu, which is the central image
and concept of the Tomatis Sound Therapy. (We aren't
told what happened to that particular autistic child, but
others appear to have been aided by the filtered sounds.)

Tomatis says: "By means of filtered sounds through
the medium of a memorized ancient audition, we arouse
the awakening of the most archaic relationship desired:
the relationship with the mother. There is no doubt possible. It shall be found in utero. In order to awaken this
same process, we provoke a revival of this very first
audition."

The result of this work is an effective treatment for

children with problems of learning, communication and perception. The therapist records the mother's voice, filtered to high frequency, reading a story which the child will like. This is then relayed to the child through the Electronic Ear.

A therapist says: "One would have to be present at these unforgettable sessions in order to fully grasp the impact of such a venture. Hearing the filtered maternal voice, the child changes his relationship with the mother; he becomes more affectionate and closer to her, much to her great satisfaction, for she feels more loved and needed. As the session progresses there is a change in the child's behaviour, both at home and at school. The parents tell us that their child is more present, that he listens better, he understands better what is said to him, he concentrates more easily and takes a greater part in the life of the home. Because he begins to be able to analyze the sound messages that come his way, the universe becomes more comprehensible to him. We see here the importance of the discriminating power of the ear. From here on, one may consider specific teaching for such a child and expect the integration of such notions as rules of grammar. He is then able to learn in half an hour what his mother or his teacher had tried for several years to make him learn."

Tomatis does say that when it is impossible to record the mother's voice, one may simply proceed with the filtered music training. A variety of problems have yielded to the therapy cassettes in the short while they have been in use; and the usage increases as they are shown to be of value to the troubled and the healthy alike. Sister

Miriam of St. Peter's tells of dining with a family who provided Walkmans and therapy cassettes for each of their three children. The children come in from playing and reach for the headphones instead of turning on the television. They enjoy the filtered music, as most children will if it isn't forced on them. In this instance it is used as prevention rather than cure.

Play itself is an important element of protection against disorders. Research has shown that cortical and sub-cortical activities must be in balance for keeping the organism stable. Children receive an overdose of cortical burdening, because they have little free time and increasing school loads. School demands cortical activity for nine-tenths of the time spent there. It's not natural for children to subordinate their sub-cortical activity to cortical control for long hours of the day. For the growing child the one-sided overburdening of the cortex may cause irreparable damage. The increase of childhood hypertensions and neurosis give warning about the need for much more recreation and freedom.

The reading disability known as dyslexia has become a modern plague. The problem was hardly known in the last generation. Today it is running rampant and is said to affect the lives of more than half the population. The dyslexic child is one who has reading difficulties that are incompatible with his or her intellectual potential. Such children are usually considered to be slow learners, and are perhaps even labelled stupid or retarded. Bright children can be indistinguishable from the less gifted: they don't like school, they hate learning, they can't concentrate, they refuse to exert an effort. If their condition is unchecked they will grow into dissatisfied and frustrated adults whose occupations will never come up to their potentials.

Tomatis has successfully treated more than 12,000 dyslexics in centres which he has established in Europe and Africa. He says: "We read with our ears." A child may be dyslexic before ever encountering the written word. Reading is not a mechanical process of decoding symbols. Children are not naming letters when they read, but rather are listening to their own voice, whether reading silently or aloud. They are also listening to what the author has to say. Reading is essentially communicating, and children will not be able to communicate if there is a failure of listening.

Listening is not the same as hearing. Listening is a voluntary act. A lack of desire to communicate causes many children with perfectly acute hearing to shut off their ears to the spoken word. A mother says: "If I talk to my son in a normal voice he doesn't hear. But when I repeat the words in a low booming voice, he looks up right away."

The child has deafened himself in the high frequencies. This we have all done in varying degrees and for reasons which are many and individual. It starts at the very beginning of life. On the tenth day after birth, from the moment when the eustachian tube empties its liquid, the infant becomes plunged into sonoric darkness, which prevents it from hearing the elevated frequencies that it heard during its foetal life. It doesn't yet know how to tense its musculature (the tympanus) in the air medium to recover its perception of the very high frequencies. The ear will have to carry on the work of accommodation and concentration for many years in order to retrieve the high levels needed for communication. In many instances the child falls short of this recovery. This is one reason why wise and informed child care is so vital in the early years. The human species is characterized by the elasticity of the central nervous system, and children are born with an opening of the inner ear diaphram from 16 cycles to about 20,000 or more. This is the range of sound perception that is available to them. But in their life experience they will settle down to cater to those frequencies which they find useful or indispensable to their immediate environment. Although possessing a wide range 'keyboard' of the inner ear, they do not necessarily use it all; by using only what is useful for them they restrict their range.

One important function of the inner ear is to supress visceral or self-produced sounds so that attention can be paid to external sounds. The tympanus is either relaxed and deaf to external stimuli, or properly tensed to tune in to the outside input. In children whose inner needs are not met, their attention will remain attached to the internal world of the viscera, and interest in the outside world will be hampered. Outside sounds, such as the spoken word, will have an emotional connotation for the child that may well be quite separate from the meaning of the words themselves. The speaker will be perceived as reassuring or threatening. The child will respond by tuning the person in or out, according to the affective message the voice holds. In negative situations the child will shut off the ear to the analysis and discrimination of speech sounds, being either too frightened by the message that is conveyed or too preoccupied with the inner visceral sounds. Hearing, therefore, becomes a matter not simply of sound, but of the way in which the message inherent in the sound is interpreted by the listener.

Children learn to tune out their parents, and when they get to school they begin tuning out the teacher by the same process. Selectivity, meaning the ability to select from the full range of sounds, is by then blocked, either on all frequencies, right and left, or on only one part of the sound scale for both ears, or for one ear only. There is another way of withdrawing from auditory communication and from entering the world of grown-ups through language, and that is by lowering the threshold of one's hearing to the point of deafness. One of the standard complaints of parents and teachers is that so many children do not listen. The problem lies in a non-listening attitude. These children lack motivation and are unable to discriminate sounds. Another trick consists in shuffling the cards, to no longer know where sound comes from, to live in confusion. There is no earthly use in nagging such children to tidy up their rooms; that only adds to the chaos in their heads and aggravates their difficulty in spatialization.

Then there is the child who chooses to keep others at a distance by choosing the longer circuits, that is by borrowing the left auditory route. The left hemisphere of the brain is the centre of symbolic thought and language, and the right ear is the most direct route to this centre. For efficient analysis of language, the right ear must be the directing ear. The left ear has to use a longer, less efficient route, and when neither ear consistently leads we see the phenomenon of reversals. For example, in the word **saw,** if the 's' is 'heard' by the left ear and the 'w' is heard by the right, the 'w' will reach the left hemisphere before the 's' and the child will read **was.**

In the treatment of dyslexia, then, not only is the filtered music used to open the ear to the full range of frequencies, but lateralization to the right is developed. This is done by continually feeding more sound into the right ear than the left. Dr. Tomatis found that when he put earphones on the children and increased the sound to the right ear, they spoke more eagerly, their reading ability improved, and their behaviour improved as well.

Tomatis's theory of auditory laterality, or the dominance of the right ear, was developed through intensive experiments with singers. It resulted in his First Law: *the voice contains only what the ear hears;* or, more scientifically: *the larynx emits only the harmonics that the ear can hear.*

He had his subjects sing and monitor themselves with both ears through headphones, while he made a sonogram which pictured a normal, well timbred, sonorous voice. Next, Tomatis "tuned out" the right ear electronically (by leaving it out of the circuit) thus forcing the subjects to listen and monitor themselves through the left ear. The subsequent diagram showed the disappearance of an entire series of harmonics. At the same time the singers found themselves slowing down; they noted that they were tired; they felt oppressed and had trouble singing in tune. Next, the singers monitored themselves with the right ear, that is they blocked out the sound of the left as it returned to them through the earphones. The diagram which resulted showed an impressive display of harmonics, even greater in content than the one where the self-monitoring was done through both ears. The subjects said that they found it very pleasant to sing in this way, and they could do it with greater facility than usual. They felt light and had a sense of well-being; the oppressed feeling had disappeared. The improvement in the voice, both in timbre and pitch, was obvious to the experimenter's ears.

Tomatis states categorically that great voices, sung or spoken, are the voices directed and controlled by the right ear and never by the left.

The same experiment performed with actors showed that speaking while monitoring with the left ear caused difficulties with timbre, concentration, attention, expression of thoughts, and finally a great tendency to fatigue. Further investigation proved conclusively that deficiencies of the voice are related to deficiencies of the ear. By systematically comparing the hearing and speech curves of subjects suffering from scotomas, Tomatis was able to show that there is an exact and total correspondence for all frequencies shown on the audiogram and phonogram: that is, of the sounds heard and the sounds emitted. When, through training with Sound Therapy, the frequencies that have been lost are restored to the ear, those frequencies are instantaneously and unconsciously restored to the voice.

Thus he earned the profound gratitude of many singers and actors. The enhancement of range and harmonics in the voice is also a great boon to teachers — and those who have to listen to them. In fact, as we speak to each other, we are exerting an immense influence over them and upon ourselves. When we speak we use an instrument which surrounds us — the air. The aerial medium is full of life; all the molecules which surround us have a speed, called relative mean speed, and this is a permanent excitation, a pressure affecting our entire body. The instant we speak or hear a sound, the air changes in its state of pressure; it becomes physically modified and begins to caress the whole body, as when we are in the bath and agitate the water and the body feels it. Every time we speak, we flood our neurons, and, on the basis of acoustic pressure, we integrate all the information that we send. To speak and to speak well gives us enormous awareness of our body as a whole, and also affects the body of the listener. Nothing is as penetrating as someone else's voice. A voice either attacks or caresses the other's being. It enters through all the pores by pressure over the entire body, as well as through the apparatus of the ear.

Those who speak well have achieved what Tomatis calls right ear dominance. His experiments in laterality were not limited to the voice, but included virtuoso performers, especially violinists. The results were the same as with the singers. When forced to monitor themselves with the left ear, they lost their ability to play well and accurately. They were hampered in their movements, which stiffened and became slower. One said to Tomatis: "Not only am I hindered in my playing, but more than that, my fingers are paralyzed."

Such observations caused Tomatis to notice the delay in rhythm which led to stuttering, and he began working with stutterers. He says: "I had about 74 stutterers and I lived with them for a year. My biggest problem was not to start stuttering. All of the stutterers had trouble hearing from the right, and all of them, when I started them using the right ear alone, began to speak correctly.'' Later he used the same system in treating children with speech difficulties, and found that not only their speech but their behaviour changed; they became more dynamic, more open and eager to talk, and the parents reported that they had improved in their reading.

Dr. E. Spirig of the Anvers Centre, Belgium, gives demonstrations of this at the Centre, using electronic equipment to produce the same reactions in volunteers chosen from among their visitors. He states: "By having volunteers read for a certain length of time while monitoring themselves with the *left* ear, we have been able to produce magnificent experimental dyslexics."

Children with listening difficulties are often seen to have poor posture. These are helped both mentally and physically by the therapy, for the main nerves affected are the auditory nerve which dynamizes the cortex, and the vestibular nerve which determines posture. The two nerves interact in a complementary way; each time the cortex is charged by picking up high frequency sounds through the ear, the vestibular nerve is influenced and improves the body schema.

Dr. Spirig writes: "If we observe children who are retarded in language, or children who stutter, or are mentally defective, we find they have stooped or curved backs. It does little good to remind them a dozen times a day to stand up straight. These children receive too little charging of the cortex, too little stimulation of the vestibular nerve. They have the look of a beaten dog. Only

an auditory re-education by means of the Electronic Ear
will bring about a permanent change in their posture.
They become vertical through language.''

Similar work is being done with spastic children, who
tend to have great psychological problems. Intensive training by means of the Electronic Ear enables doors to open
which until now have been blocked by enormous
inhibitions.

The raising of the hearing threshold to normal level,
and its re-awakening of the desire to communicate, demonstrates again and again the degree to which deficiencies are related to blockages of the ear. We live most of
our lives unaware of these obstructions which impede our
motivation and disrupt our communication with each other. Those who have not experienced the listening cannot
realize what they are missing by keeping their distortions.
It is so easy to hear and to communicate once the ear is
open to the external world, and so difficult to relate har-
moniously to the environment when one must constantly correct, on the cortical level, the distortions that com-
plicate existence.

Whenever laterality is discussed, the question of left-
handedness arises. It is generally agreed in these circles
that it is better to be right-handed than left. It's not that
left-handed people are not as smart or as capable of
achievement, but the same degree of achievement would
seem to require more effort, due to their having to use
longer circuits. To see that life is harder for them, you
only have to watch a lefty in the excruciating act of
writing. I can say that, because I am one myself. The
general coercion of my school days began with my being

compelled to switch over from my left to my right —
perhaps because I wrote my name, Pat, as Tap. The
changeover may have been a good thing, though Tap
Joudry on my books might have been an eye catcher and
helped them move. Psychologists later put a stop to the
practice, claiming it would cause stuttering; although according to Tomatis, stuttering was more likely to result
from leaving things as they were. At any rate, all my life
since, I have written with my right hand and stubbornly
done everything else with my left, and the only time I stutter is when the bank manager calls.

Tomatis, whose coerciveness is more subtle, not to
mention more beneficial, asked himself one day whether
one might make lefties right-handed without letting them
know, by working on their ear. He finally decided to take
the step with one of his own children, three of whom were
left-handed. He worked on his son's right ear, and at a
certain point, spontaneously, the boy changed to the right
hand. His efficiency and speed of learning also increased,
and his speech became more controlled.

Tomatis says: "When I treat the right ear, it sometimes happens that the left-handed child starts mixing his
handedness: he is hesitant. I encourage him by saying that
he is not giving up his left hand, but that it has other tasks
to perform. For a while he is disconcerted because his
right hand is a clumsy instrument. But in a very short
while it takes over, and there is no more confict."

He tells us also that laterality is very labile, and gives
an example which occured at an industrial depot, where
he was doing tests with workers' hearing. "At the depot
the majority were right-handed. As the people work on

jets they are engaged in precision work and subject to a high level of fatigue. On Monday morning they are all right-handed; Thursday and Friday evening, before they quit work, they are casualties of mixed laterality; they are neither right nor left-handed. At that point they are also hesitant to talk to anybody. They feel that their apparatus of feedback is not functioning properly. If one gave them a rifle for trial, I am sure they would not be able to aim at a target either. All their aiming potential has been damaged.''

The military minded might see in this therapy a system to improve the accuracy of a soldier's aim. It would work the other way, of course, and abolish aggression by awakening the higher, conscious self. The left brain zones of communication and awareness are responsible for the desire to grow, to live, to accept autonomy and joyous responsibility for one's own actions; they represent the fusion of the life instinct and the death instinct, and thus give the life impulse its victory.

Chapter Four

Sleep

Tomatis believes that the need for sleep is exaggerated. As the cortex needs constant energy inputs via sensory intake, and most people don't have enough stimulating activities, he thinks they turn to sleep as an escape and a refuge.

Other scientists are starting to ask whether we have to sleep at all. James M. Kruger, assistant professor of physiology at Chicago Medical School, says: "For all we know, we don't need sleep. If we had a drug that blocked the effect of the sleep factor in the brain, we might be able to stay awake twenty-four hours a day without ill effects."

It is generally agreed that sleep has a restorative function. But what is it restoring, the body or the brain? Muscle can shut down its activity and reach roughly the same level of recovery during human wakefulness as it can in sleep. Tests conducted with subjects deprived of sleep for periods as long as 8 - 11 days showed few ill effects. The physiological ability to do physical work would be expected to decrease during deprivation if sleep were essential to muscle restitution, but tests using this measure over three to five sleepless days reported no change.

The cerebral cortex, where our most complex mental activities go on, is often considered to be the part of the brain most in need of sleep. However, Dr. Bob Wilkinson of the Applied Psychology Unit in Cambridge has demonstrated in a variety of studies that a whole range of "cerebrally demanding," complex, decision-making tasks, such as chess playing, battle games and IQ tests, are not notably affected by sleep deprivation. These can be maintained at near normal levels for several days. It is the mundane and prolonged tasks, like reacting to simple light stimuli, which are the first to fall. It seems that the key to overcoming any drop in performance is to have sufficient motivation to offset the effects of sleeplessness. If it matters enough, one can usually perform it. Cerebrally demanding work is inherently interesting, unlike the simple tasks, and if subjects have an added incentive for doing well, they have shown they can maintain performance at a good level.

This is what prompts Tomatis to say that we sleep instead of engaging in stimulating activity. The brain depends upon recharging. Whereas the rest of the body needs nourishment, the brain is almost a separate element. You can starve an individual to death, and his flesh and bones will lose weight substantially, whereas the brain loses hardly any weight, a mere two per cent. It is stimulation which feeds the brain. "The more we think, the less we need to rest."

One of the findings from the sleep-deprivation tests was that our deepest sleep is the most essential, with the lighter, REM (for Rapid Eye Movement) or dreaming sleep being somewhat optional. Sleep follows a cyclical pattern throughout the night, with REM sleep appearing in increasing quantities every 90 minutes. Deep sleep is usually confined to the first three cycles, declining in quantity over these cycles. After about five hours of sleep we have taken most of our deep sleep, together with about half of the REM sleep. From the sleep-deprivation findings it was deduced that the last two or three hours of our nightly sleep may be expendable, yet are well ingrained into our sleeping habits.

The two mechanisms which cause us to sleep, then, are a need for restoration (though not as much of it as we have thought) and a sleep drive to keep us occupied during darkness. There is sleep we need and sleep we can do without.

It is the unneeded sleep which falls away with Sound Therapy. The signal that the effect is taking hold is that suddenly one morning you wake up an hour or so earlier than usual. You awaken simply, peacefully, feeling deeply rested and refreshed. Odd. It's six o'clock instead of seven. You roll over from habit and go back to sleep. Next time you may wake at five, then four. All the inner signals tell you you have slept enough and can get up. But you can't believe it. The habit is strong. It tries to tug you back to sleep.

The truth is you can get up as soon as you waken in that way, coming suddenly out of sleep, feeling bright and rested. You have enough energy for the day; more than enough. By late evening you still won't feel tired, even if you've been working long and hard.

Once again the habit patterns are thrown into confusion. Do you go to bed or don't you, when you feel as though you just got up — even though it's midnight? You go to bed from a sense of duty and drift easily into sleep, without the old tossing and turning. That must mean you were worn out. Yet four or five hours later you're awake again and feeling on top of the world.

Habit tries to re-assert itself, and you want to roll over and snatch more sleep, though you know very well you do not need it. An effort is needed to get up: not an effort of the body, but an effort of the will. The body is working on a new time schedule and the inner clock has to be adjusted.

Only the insomniac appreciates to the full the blessedness of sleep. Such a sufferer would wonder at anyone wishing to reduce that gift of gifts. It can be done in this instance because the quality of sleep is changed. Ordinary sleep could not be cut by a third or a half. With the energizing and tranquilizing of the system through brain recharge, sleep is concentrated and compressed, becoming doubly efficient. It is deep and pure and thorough, like a child's slumber.

The medical name for this kind of sleeping is hypersomnia. It is the exact opposite of in-somnia. Insomnia is caused by cortical excitation, hypersomnia by cortical inhibition — a healthy inhibition. While you are up and around the relaxing effect of the therapy manifests itself in tranquility of mind, a sense of well-being and imperviousness to stress; when you lie down and shift your mind into the sleep gear, you sink sweetly away. The fact that you have not accumulated tiredness through the day contributes to the ease and refreshment of the sleep.

One woman, hearing how the brain recharge reduces the need for sleep, was horrified. "You want to rob me of half my sleep?" she cried. "I have enough trouble killing time as it is."

So be warned: Sound Therapy is only for people who want more time in their lives, because as sure as you listen you are going to get it. After a short period of adjustment it will become the natural thing. Then if you want to have a Sunday morning lie-in for old times' sake, go ahead. You won't be sleepy and the extra rest won't do you any good, but as the doctors say about vitamins, it won't hurt you.

Time is money, we are told. But time is something better than that. It is growth. More time means more life. There's a feeling of richness about having abundant time. It takes a pressure off the heart; no more does the correspondence pile up and the books you want to read sit nagging on the shelf. The quiet hours of darkness, when the house and street and air lanes are still, is a marvellous time for creative work, for learning a language, for studying the other things you always wanted to know. When the family comes stumbling down the stairs to breakfast, you have just hit your stride. At night when they're knocked out, you're still waiting to get tired. And you're going to have a long wait. After a while you can't remember what tiredness was. It's like the dim memory of an ancient illness.

Yet at first it's disconcerting to find yourself sitting

in the living room with your cup of coffee at three or four in the morning, looking at the black windows and feeling that the sun has forgotten to come up.

You feel like asking your mother, "What am I going to **do?**" You know what she'd say. "Think of something."

You have to think of quite a few things. The remaining part of your life has been lengthened by approximately one sixth. If you are, say, forty, with forty more to go, you have received a gift of about six years. They can be the fullest years of all, because your mental faculties are also expanded.

For myself, the choice of reading material had always been restricted because I found so many subjects boring: a legacy from school. Especially I couldn't care about politics and history. Then one day a door quietly opened, and I became avid for politics and history. Tucking into Winston Churchill's six massive volumes on the Second World War, I found it the adventure story of the century. Next came Solzhenitsyn's horror story, **The Gulag Archipelago.** These monumental works yielded easily to the abundance of time and new receptivity of mind. Now all of history beckons. It's like opening the catacombs and scooping up the buried treasure.

I wouldn't place a bet now on what doors are permanently closed. It's not natural to have any part of the mind boarded up. And conscious or unconscious, opening doors never let in any spooks. Things only have power to fright when they're locked out.

And look, the sun is rising.

Chapter Five

How To Listen

First, don't listen. Do something else and let the music happen without too much conscious attention — though if you want to pause and listen now and then, there's no harm in that.

You don't have to embroider doilies or underemploy your intelligence with jig-saw puzzles, though when you want to relax with such activities, it's a very good time to do the listening. In the main you just play the music while carrying on with your day. Listen at home, on the way to work — driving, walking or taking the bus — maybe even on the job, though it's likely to be more acceptable with some kinds of jobs than others. Now that the students at St. Peter's College are listening with their Sony Walkmans five hours a day in the classrooms, the teachers are free to do the same; but don't look for it yet in the average school.

If you're self employed, you're home free. A Saskatoon stereo repairman listens most of the day at his bench;

so does a goldsmith. A chiropractor uses it while doing his adjustments and doesn't need an adjustment himself any more at the end of the day.

To listen while reading is to impress the words more firmly on the mind, and so it's ideal for study. You can listen at meals or in coffee breaks. Try playing it at imperceptible volume while watching TV; it will give protection against that dragged-out feeling and leave you alert enough to do something useful afterwards.

For the homemaker it lightens the hours at the stove and sink, clipped to the belt or carried around in a fabric shoulderbag, or else slung about the neck. It's useful at the sewing machine or typewriter, to counteract the sound of the motor; particularly when using the vacuum cleaner or electric mixer. When the kids get too rowdy, promise them ten minutes' listening each. This should always be treated as a special privilege for children, never applied under compulsion; it's too good to ruin. It has a profound effect on the young, forming mind, and therefore is most valuable of all for pregnant women. People claim to have produced genius children by the use of Sound Therapy throughout pregnancy. Never mind genius: it's enough if the embryonic brain forms to its best advantage.

If you're a meditator you'll find it a great benefit in meditation, taking you into the deep state more easily and quickly. An excellent time to use it is after a meal, when the blood leaves the brain for the digestive system and ordinarily makes you tired; the brain recharge will eliminate the tiredness and also aid digestion due to the relaxation it gives. Play it while resting, and at night when going to sleep. If you like to read in bed, take your Walkman with you, and you'll soon fall asleep over your book, half waking a little later to remove the headphones and put out the light. The time that it plays during sleep is the most beneficial of all, as the sound flows unobstructedly into the unconscious mind. And you don't have to press Stop. It goes off by itself.

Keep the volume between low and medium. It does just as much good at faint volume as louder. Since it has the effect of opening the hearing, you will find yourself reducing the volume as time goes on.

Any kind of sound at too high a level will damage the ear. We hear of young people these days destroying their hearing — what's left of it from the discos — by playing portable cassette players at top volume. This is why people will tell you that it's dangerous to drive a car with headphones on. If you can't hear the sounds around you, of course it is. But to play the Sound Therapy cassette at low volume makes you a safer driver. It induces relaxation and keeps you alert, while still allowing you to hear the outside sounds.

And here is an important point. When you have your Walkman set to where you can just hear it, and you start your car or step out into the noise of the street, *do not turn the volume up*. You don't have to be able to hear the music; it is still going into your ears and doing its work. It never has to compete with other sounds.

Another reason for keeping the volume low is that you will realize all the sooner how easy it is to communicate with people and conduct all the business of your life while getting in your listening hours. At first you'll encounter resistance. People will think you're shutting them out. Simply explain that this sound is very gentle, and offer them the headphones so that they can try it.

I have found that to listen while travelling brings me to my destination without a trace of tiredness. The cause of the exhaustion that usually accompanies travel is the barrage of discharging sounds that attacks the system from the minute you enter the airport. Airports and railway stations are thick with low frequency sounds: the hum of machinery, fluorescent lights, computers, luggage carts, P.A. announcements. The plane interior emits an aggressive low frequency noise that systematically drains energy from the brain. Though the high frequency music is a faint sound in comparison, it will counteract these insidious drones, and bear us above the damage as surely as the plane itself carries us high over the earth.

Wear your Walkman while shopping, unless you care what people think. If public opinion worries you, you won't be into this anyway. People may shout at you when you're wearing the headphones, but if you speak calmly back they'll get the idea.

As word gets around about the use of the Walkman in the classrooms at St. Peter's, the listening therapy has begun to make its way into other schools. An open and receptive attitude on the part of a few principals, teachers and parents has resulted in certain children being able to take a Walkman and therapy tapes to school with them. They listen at their desks for most of the day, and reports indicate better learning, less stress, and improved behaviour both at school and at home.

And here a question arises. Some parents ask: ''If

I buy my child a Walkman, how do I know that he/she is not going to use it to listen to rock music?"

The anxiety is understandable. The effect of rock music, at the volume that it is ordinarily played, is now known to damage hearing, and certainly is no aid to study. Yet the answer is simple. There are many destructive elements in this world and most of them represent one side of a coin whose other side is positive and constructive. The more beneficial a thing is, the greater its negative power is likely to be. Sound is one example; the sun is another; Creation itself has a shadow side. Wherever destructive possibility exists it exists for the purpose of being met, counteracted and overcome.

Parents universally complain about the effect of pop music on the young. But who is doing anything about it? No one is educating young people in the effects of sound, both harmful and beneficial. Almost no one is introducing them to the wealth of classical music that exists in the world and which will enrich their whole lives, once admitted to consciousness. To say, "Well, I'm not going to introduce my children to good sound because they might make wrong use of the cassette player" is to admit defeat before even trying a better way.

It is a fact that parents have been helpless before the onslaught of musical noise. Here at last is a chance to meet this threat, to educate children on matters of sound at an early age. It means granting them a measure of personal responsibility, a positive gesture in itself, and one which usually results in more good than harm.

To provide children with the means of hearing beneficial sound is not bound to encourage them in the opposite direction. At any rate, to withhold it is no protection. They are going to listen to rock music anyway, if not on their own cassette player, on someone else's. They're going to have their eardrums blasted at discos or simply walking along the downtown streets. The only real protection lies in informing them and equipping them with a method of healing and safeguarding their precious hearing.

Sister Miriam at St. Peter's tells how the first students to be introduced to the Walkmans on their desks were thrilled to death, and turned up the next day with handfuls of rock music cassettes. She saw that they had missed the point. She explained: "If you listen to Sound Therapy music for fifteen minutes and then listen to rock for the same length of time, it will undo the good effect of the Sound Therapy and take away a little something as well."

The students were interested in hearing that. No one had ever explained such a thing to them. Most had never listened to classical music in their lives. They not only got used to it very quickly, but many grew to like it. They wanted to take the cassettes home to listen to on their home stereo systems, and a rotating library of Sound Therapy cassettes was set up. It proves again that as all the impulses of the body are toward healing, so is the direction of the mind. It only needs to be informed. To explain the differences in the values of sound, and allow young people — even very young people — a measure of choice, cannot fail to weigh the scales on the side of health.

Another question has been asked. "Are my children

going to sleep less if they do this therapy? Will they start getting up at four in the morning . . . and refuse to go to bed at night?''

The answer is No. Parents of children who are on the therapy say there is no problem with this. The listening results in a balancing and harmonizing of the person at whatever age. Adults are relieved of stress; kids calm down. Men and women who have been sleeping longer hours than the body really requires will sleep less. Hyperactive children who have been sleeping very little begin to sleep more. Other children may have been over-sleeping as an escape from emotional problems, and these will move toward normalcy with respect to behaviour and hours of sleep. Children need more sleep than adults, and therefore, when in health, will sleep a correct length of time. The Sound Therapy will merely assure that the sleep is fully restorative.

How long should you listen? There is no limit to the time that you *may* listen. Three hours a day is prescribed in the formal therapy, and I have found that length of time to be effective with people using my Walkman system. I recommend three hours *minimum,* because those who find they can manage four or five hours appear to have results sooner. Once people get into the habit of simply wearing the Walkman around, and it registers that they really can do everything else while listening, it's no more bother to listen five hours than five minutes. A teacher tells me, ''In the morning I put on my clothes and my Walkman along with them. It's more trouble to take it off than leave it on. I soon forget I'm wearing it.''

The listening does not have to be done at one stretch

but can be spread out over the day and evening as convenient. It is better, in fact, to have a few breaks, to do some vocalizing — humming, singing or even talking — as the voice is also an instrument of recharge.

How long will it take? The length of time varies with each individual. The Tomatis sound therapist, by applying the listening test, can read the results on the audiogram and see the degree to which the ear's selectivity is blocked. He can then foretell with some degree of accuracy the length of time required for the opening. With self therapy, we don't know until it happens. As a general rule, 100 to 200 hours of listening are necessary before the effect begins to be felt. A few people require less; some take longer; but if you persist there is no doubt that it will have its result.

Until the opening occurs, it's essential that you put in the hours daily. Once you've achieved the breakthrough, and the new energy patterns are firmly established, you can vary the listening time as you wish. When the ear is about to open, there's a signal. You get terribly tired. Father Lawrence has come up with a good image: "You might picture the brain at this stage as being like a bowl of jelly, held in the hands and very gently shaken." The pathways are being subtly rearranged, and as they settle into new and more harmonious patterns the newfound energy is released. The tiredness may last for a week, a little more, a little less. It's a very relaxed condition, usually coming on in the evening, and you just sleep it off. It is the last tiredness you will ever know, if you continue the regular recharging.

In most cases this tiredness precedes the inrush of

vitality, but some people have been known to get the energy first and the tiredness later — or not at all. There is a period, on the cusp of change, when you should refrain from playing the music while driving, for you could drop off to sleep. There could also at some point be a slight aching of the ears; this is due to bone conduction of the sound. It's a sign that the Electronic Ear is changing the nature of the auditory system and is a good sign. It will soon pass. Some people report a touch of dizziness from time to time, and this passes too.

The great difference in the speed with which people respond is due to a number of factors, such as the extent to which selectivity is blocked, and also whether the person is an audio or visual type. Some people relate to the world through their ears, and others through their eyes, and there are extremes and variants of these. A purely audio type is likely to experience the opening of the ear much faster than the visual person. Musicians are already halfway there, in contrast to visual artists, whose ears can be very stubborn.

This is because visual people tend to be "right brained" — more strongly influenced by the right hemisphere, where the spatial sense is located. As the right hemisphere is influenced by the left ear, such people are more comfortable with a predominance of sound to the left rather than the right. They are sometimes very resistant to the Sound Therapy music with its right ear emphasis, and when nobody's looking might switch the headphones around!

The left hemisphere, in the overwhelming majority of people, contains the centres for language, memory, concentration, and the active force for the release of energy. The hemispheres are equal in importance, but their activities are different. The right hemisphere may be visualized as the instrument, with the left taking the role of virtuoso, or the one which executes. The right hemisphere is marked by a force which is receptive, while the left is invested with consciousness and activity and becomes the dynamic representative of the central nervous system.

Writers, and people dealing in language and symbolic thought, appear to respond more quickly than others to the opening of the auditory system through this therapy. Yet it may be that those whose ear is slower to open are in need of it most. Their selectivity may be blocked on all frequencies. Little by little the uncultivated areas have to be cleared and brought to life. Though it takes longer, the end result will be all the more gratifying and worthwhile.

Technical aptitudes are a function of the right hemisphere, and in my own case, I can only consider that for most of my life my right brain was pretty well out of commission. I was hopeless at drawing, couldn't do math, had no spatial sense, tending to misjudge distances and bump into things as I made my way around. The radical effect of the therapy on my grasp of things technical indicates clearly how the sound, though directed to the left hemisphere, affects the brain in its entirety. It would also seem to conform to Tomatis' statement that, due to the differing lengths of the circuits, stimulation directed to the left hemisphere reaches the right by a shorter route than if fed to the right, via the left ear.

Therefore we are encouraged to tend the right ear to all sounds. In conversation, try to seat yourself so that the other person's voice comes from your right. I leave it to you to imagine the fun when two sound therapists start jockeying for position!

About the tapes: All are recorded with right ear dominance, so it's important to put the headphone marked R to the right ear. After a time this emphasis begins to sound natural, and your normal tapes, with equal balance, seem rather strange.

Most of the tapes are filtered to ascending frequency, starting at normal, rising to 6,000 or 8,000 Hz, leveling out for a while and then returning to normal. This aids the ear in tuning itself gradually to the high frequency sound. Once adjusted, it can accomodate a steady 8,000 Hz, and some tapes maintain that frequency all the way through. The 8K (8 kilohertz) is valuable when you want a quicker recharge, but isn't as interesting to hear as the ones with more frequency range.

Variety is an essential factor in our lives. Listening to this for three hours a day makes it essential to have a wide choice of music. The program should never be attempted with a single tape: after listening to it daily for a week, you'd never want to hear it again. The first tapes are being issued to the public in a set of four. These are 90 minute metal tapes, and should be played at the metal setting on your Walkman. New selections will be brought out from time to time, so that the Sound Therapy music may be added to, like any collection.

Though the filtering varies on the tapes, they are recorded from first to last through the Electronic Ear, and it is this device which distinguishes Sound Therapy from several other high frequency systems, or simple Music Therapies. It is the 'rocking effect' of the Electronic Ear which exercises the middle ear and opens the auditory system to the full range of frequencies. Somewhat similar is the Bates method of strengthening the muscles of the eyes through exercise. Very few people are willing to stick with those exercises, because they're boring. They're something you have to *do*, whereas the Electronic Ear does this for you. Its unique sound is detectable on the tape as a faint, intermittent hissing, rather like snow striking a window. It may detract from the purity of the sound, but is doing a world of good, and so the sound has to sacrifice a little. Above all, don't try to lessen it with the Dolby button! Dolby should never be used for the Sound Therapy tapes, as it involves a loss of frequency at the top.

The tapes are made on equipment with a frequency response of 20,000 hertz. Therefore, if you happen to have a quality tape deck at home, such as the Sony TC K777 with a 20,000 frequency response, and a good set of headphones, you can take advantage of the added frequency when you want to just settle down in the living room.

Equipment: The Sony Walkman is recommended for Sound Therapy, as most other makes do not have the required high frequency response. Among the many Sony models, choose one with 15,000 or 16,000 Hz top. Sony is continually bringing out new models, and you should check the Specifications in the booklet before making your choice.

The Sony headphones are made to accomodate the 16,000 Hz response, and one should never use phones of a lower calibre, for the frequencies will not be conveyed. If you buy a cheap cassette player you're wasting your time doing the therapy.

The listening must be done with headphones, though it is possible to play the cassettes through speakers and derive a slight benefit. It might be tried in a room where children are playing. As children are particularly responsive, they may get almost as much from it as an adult with closed hearing listening through phones.

The Walkman should be cared for as conscientiously as any good stereo player, the heads cleaned (with alcohol, not a cleaning tape) at regular intervals, and also demagnetized frequently. This will preserve the high frequency capacity on the tapes. With such steady use the headphone plugs may start to wear; you'll know this if the sound to one ear cuts out. The plugs are sold separately in stereo stores and can be changed. If in the changing, the tiny wires happen to get crossed, you will find you have left ear dominance instead of right, and it will have to be corrected. Listening for this provides good practice in awareness of right/left separation.

You go through a lot of batteries, so it pays to buy a battery recharger and the special rechargeable batteries that go with it. The charger is plugged into a wall outlet; it holds four batteries and these require eight to twenty hours of charging, depending upon which kind of charger you have. You need two sets of batteries, because you are using one set while another is charging. There are adaptors on the market which will enable you to play your

Walkman through a wall outlet; but many of these have a hum, so be sure to get a Sony adaptor. It's also possible, if you know something about wiring, to hook the Walkman up to the lighter socket in your car.

If two people in the house are doing the therapy, they shouldn't try to share a Walkman — or even a battery charger. The main feature of the self therapy is the freedom to listen when you choose, and relationships could come to grief through wrestling over the equipment.

The time comes when the effect is more or less permanent; the auditory system has been changed and acts, as it were, like a dynamo recharging the central battery, which in turn distributes energy to the whole nervous system. You will have learned to tune into the high frequencies wherever they exist. Linda Anderson, the writer, says: "I'm charged by everything now — my regular music, my own voice, the voices of others, bird songs and the sound of rain . . ."

You can then suit yourself as to how much listening you want to do. Extra demands on your energy can be met by putting on the high frequency music. While there is a consistently higher energy state, there's no reason to suppose that that level cannot be steadily lifted by continued use of the music. Some people become so fond of the sound that they choose to go on listening to it every day, and look forward to doing it for the rest of their lives. The effect appears to be cumulative. As the energy level maintains its high state and imperceptibly rises, the relaxation deepens into a yogic serenity, an imperviousness to stress.

Once the auditory opening has occurred, there is a

little technique for using your new long days to fullest effect. When you feel yourself slowing down, sit (or lie) back with a book and your Walkman and read to the music. Your eyes will grow heavy; very soon they will close and you'll sink down into a mini-sleep which may only be two or three minutes but will be as refreshing as an hour. You will awaken fully alert, with none of the hungover, groggy feeling that usually follows a daytime sleep. Doing this occasionally, you will find that you never have to come to a long full stop — that is, unless you want to.

But at the start there are two rules that can't be emphasized too much. The listening must be done regularly. "Spot listening," picking it up now and then, is useless. To do it halfway will not give half results: it will give no results at all. Compare it with a weight lifter lifting weights. The muscles must have the daily, unremitting exercise if they are to develop. It is the same with the development of the middle ear muscles, those which bring about the transformation in listening and cause all the rest to happen.

Secondly: **Don't look for quick results.** Allow two to four months before expecting to notice any change. The occasional person takes much longer. It is a process, a re-education of the ear, not Aladdin's lamp. Some people put on the headphones for five minutes and say, "It isn't doing anything for me." That's like picking up a foreign language textbook and flipping through it with your thumb and saying, "I can't speak the language yet." The new language of frequencies has to be acquired, and the rates of speed are as individual as individuals themselves. Some listen for a month or two and then fall into discouragement because someone else made the break-through in half the time. The other person was probably predominantly left-brained, an audio type, and lacked the childhood traumas that contribute so much to clos-ing off the receptivity of the ear. The longer it takes for the ear to open to the recharging effect of the high fre-quencies, the more the life force has been dammed up and the more essential it is to release it. Only the very exceptional person starts responding within a few weeks. Everyone wants to be exceptional, so will hope to fall in-to that category. If you're doing Sound Therapy at all, you are exceptional enough.

The initial effect *can* be dramatic, but don't count on it. More often than not it's a gradual thing. The new energy comes creeping in; the expanding glow is subtle. You're feeling terrific — but can you be sure of what's causing it? Skeptical people invariably cast about for every reason under the sun that might explain the unac-customed vitality and serenity. It's the moon, or some new medication, or maybe self-hypnosis . . . until the day comes when they can no longer deny that it is the Sound Therapy and nothing but the Sound Therapy. Once open-ly acknowledged, enthusiasm grows and before they know it they're trying to convert all their friends.

Recharging effect of the voice: The Hindu man-tra, OM, is based on scientific knowledge of voice vibra-tion and its energizing effect upon the brain, particular-ly the pineal gland for awakening intuition. The real value is in the end mmmmm of the OM, which sets everything vibrating, with the mouth closed and the tongue blocked inside the mouth.

The Tomatis therapy incorporates this principle in a humming technique which is introduced after the selectivity of the ear begins to open. The microphone and headphones are used, so that the voice comes back into the singer's ears, with greater volume to the right ear. Try it after a few weeks of home listening, and you'll find it will add to the effect. You hum — any tune within the mid-range of your voice, and you can test and find the best range by paying attention to the degree of vibration it sets up in your head; notes too high or too low will not cause as much vibration. The mouth should be kept closed and the lips projected forward poutingly; this eliminates tenseness at the corners of the mouth, as tenseness of these muscles inhibits the functioning of the middle ear muscles. This forward thrusting lifts the humming vibration up into the head, and you can test this too, by humming with the mouth open or the lips held normally; you will feel the difference. You can then add to the effectiveness by lightly holding the right ear closed, or even putting a little cotton into it; thus you get the right ear emphasis.

If you feel foolish — and who wouldn't? — do it while alone in the house or on solitary walks. It's good for gardening, and for walking on the beach, where you don't want to take your Walkman. And it's a lifesaver when you run out of batteries.

It would seem from this that deaf people would be very deficient in energy. It is true that they have to work harder than most of us for their supply of life force, and some are able to rise to the extra demands which are placed upon the brain, and others are not. There is a certain compensation in that the deaf are not prey to the low, discharging sounds which bombard the hearing person. But there is work to be done in exposing the hearing-impaired to high frequency pulses and also training their voices for the recharge that accompanies humming. To illustrate the importance of voice vibration, they tell the story of a silent order of monks in France. Forbidden to speak, they had always sung for six hours a day. But even monasteries have a young generation which is protesting against the old ways, and at one point the monks decided to abolish singing. They couldn't see that it had any particular purpose and was a waste of time, six hours a day and eight on Sunday. They did away with song, and right away they got tired. Investigating the cause of their exhaustion, they decided it must be their habit of early rising. They took to sleeping in in the mornings and got even more tired. They revised their diet, thinking that possibly they should start eating meat like everybody else. Their energy levels sank lower, and some months after this experiment began, Dr. Tomatis was called in.

He arrived at an abbey that contained ninety monks and found seventy of them sitting in their cells doing nothing, withdrawn like schizoid beings. He knew immediately what the problem was. With his electronic equipment he began re-educating the monks' ears and restoring the ability to sing. That was in July. By November, sixty-seven monks had begun to be active again. For the others nothing could be done; they were advanced in the disintegration of their being and ended up in a mental hospital. Their brains had become completely discharged through lack of stimulus, and could not be sparked back to life.

It makes you think. It makes you sing.

So now, knowing all the rules, you are ready to begin. But don't, we repeat don't, expect the results to be strictly by the rules. Any good therapy takes account of the differences in people, and Sound Therapy more than most allows for tremendous variations in type and speed of response. This has nothing to do with brains, or spiritual evolution either. It is simply the marvellous, mysterious uniqueness of people.

You will not necessarily experience the 'breakthrough' we speak of, but maybe only a 'creepthrough'. You may only have improved sleep (only!), or better hearing or reduced stress. It's a gamble. But whether you win a big prize or a small one, you will win something. You can't lose if you just put on the headphones and walk, man.

Father Lawrence DeMong was responsible for introduc-
ing the listening therapy at St. Peter's.

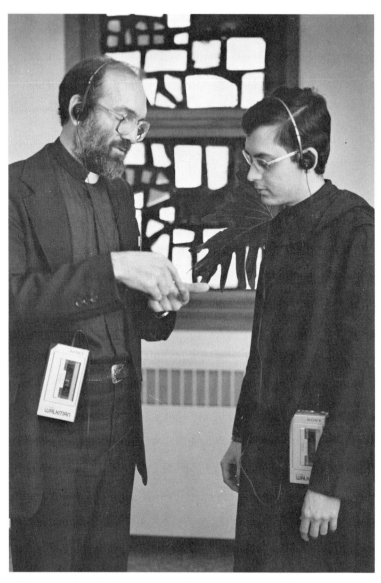

The twentieth century in the abbey. Father Lawrence, with organist and electronics expert Brother William Thurmeier.

Donna Hagel listens while serving in her store, Saskatoon Herbs 'N' Health Foodport, and tunes customers into the therapy.

Jogging to Sound Therapy means greater distances and less fatique.

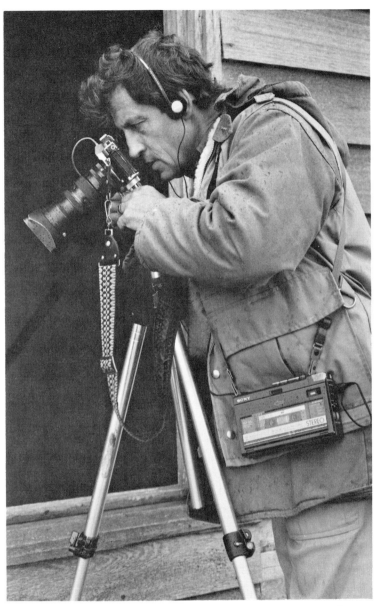

Michael Brauer, who took these photographs, finds that the music is stimulating, energizing, and encourages him to do more experimental work.

Sister Miriam Spenrath and her students at St. Peter's College listen in class and, at the very least, are much less frazzled at the end of the day than many teachers and pupils.

Catherine Lacey paints and listens. Sound Therapy helps an artist to maintain the state of relaxed alertness which induces inspiration.

Photographer Courtney Milne spends whole days on the prairie with his camera and Walkman. He says, "And then I can go home and write until 3:00 a.m. and still am not tired."

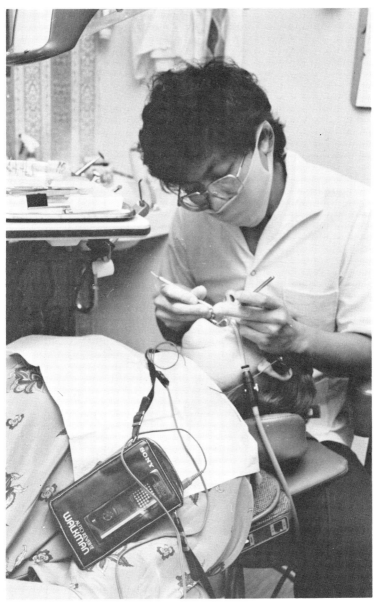

At the dentist's the therapy music removes tension and the major part of the pain, which is mental.

Chapter Six

Case Histories

Some people ask, "Have you done scientific tests with the Walkman therapy?" The answer is that it is being tested every day — not in laboratories, but in the arena of life. This is a technique which can only be proven in the doing, for every individual is different and every one responds in a unique way.

The cassettes have now been used by many hundreds of people, who have listened on their Walkmans while going about their daily routines, and recorded the results. Some of these are dramatic, some subtle. Certain effects turn up in all reports: the briefer, improved sleep; the relaxation, energy and sense of well being; also, inevitably, the improvement in hearing. Sound Therapy is of great benefit to the blind, due to its sharpening of the hearing faculty, and the protection it gives against hearing loss with ageing.

And then, many people have something uniquely theirs to add . . . asthmatic attacks allayed, sense of taste returning to one in whom it had been lost for years.

One person says: "The therapy has brought me back to God." Another asserts: "It's given sex a real boost." Is that a spread . . . or is it?

There is evidence of a change in eating habits. People tend toward healthier foods. For the overweight person, the music acts as a natural appetite suppressant; metabolism slows, stress is alleviated and the body requires less food. Or it makes more efficient use of what it receives, so that the person who is underweight can actually gain.

One clear fact emerged: everyone who followed the listening instructions faithfully reaped positive benefits; there was no person for whom the therapy did not work.

The reports are not all in, and will never be all in as long as there are unique individuals out there walking around with their headphones on. But here are a few samples chosen from many.

Dr. Cliff Bacchus, author and Member of the American Academy of Family Physicians, Governor's Harbour, Eleuthera, Bahamas:

"I was introduced to the Sound Therapy cassette system in the winter of 1983, and began listening to the music on the day that I purchased my Sony Walkman in Miami. I listened for about six hours a day during the first three days, while making my way about through the noise and confusion of that city, and also during the flight back to my island of Eleuthera. After these three days I was aware of an energy and mental clarity such as I had not experienced since before entering University, many years earlier. One notable happening during the first week was that, whereas I had never before had the patience — or stamina at the end of a day of seeing patients — to play Backgammon with my young daughter, as she constantly pleaded for me to do, I could now spend a whole evening with her at this game, wearing my headphones and listening to the therapy music. Thus, there was an immediate improvement in family harmony. After ten days of listening, there was a change in the character of my dreams. I had had great difficulty in remembering my dreams, while knowing that they usually verged on the nightmarish. Listening to the therapy music for a time before going to sleep, I began having vivid, happy dreams, with the clarity and purity of childhood dreams: sailing away on a Caribbean cruise; flying through the high air from Hawaii to Tahiti. I also remembered the dreams in detail. At the same time, my creative doors flew open. I began rising earlier in the mornings and listening to the music during several hours of creative writing, which preceded my office hours. I now sleep better, think better, write better, and am eager to get all my patients onto Sound Therapy — particularly the pregnant women, and the children with learning problems.''

Linda Taylor Anderson, Melbourne, Florida, author of **Carousing in the Kitchen:**

''My friend Patricia didn't endeavour to convince me to give Sound Therapy a try. It was my own idea. I wanted what she had: extra energy, more waking hours and blessed tranquility. That is why, as a healthy, functioning person, I incorporated sound therapy into my life.

After less than sixty hours of listening, suddenly, incredibly, new sounds were singing in my ears. I had assumed I'd always heard them, but it is amazing how much we hear, yet do not hear. I am now acutely conscious of sound, all sound, including my own voice which I can now control. Octavizing up or down is now easily accomplished. It is the sound therapy that has gifted me with this new awareness. Further amazement came. When properly energized, the body can function on very little sleep. I have always required eight hours of heavy duty sleep. Now I often wake up in the night, after only three to four hours sleep, snap my eyes open, stretch and feel ready to tackle whatever may be coming my way. I do not always rise to the occasion, preferring the comfort and warmth of the bed. But there is none of the old tossing and turning. I lie peacefully, pursuing my ranging thoughts, making promises and programs for the hours and days to come, as I am now able to concentrate my energy into a basic force that is not easily sidetracked. I see others fade; I am fresh and eager for the next encounter. If I feel the approach of tiredness, I simply lie down for a few minutes with the music and drift into rest, rising calmed, refreshed and ready to carry on.''

A year later Linda writes: "I'm still listening. Not three hours a day but at least 45 minutes. I usually listen at night; when I go to bed, on go the headphones. I go to sleep and the music plays on. When I miss a day I'm not happy about it. I feel something important is lacking. It's as though my internal batteries that provide calm, energy and a feeling of well-being just hadn't been charged. I'll never stop listening. Never is a strong word, but that's how I feel about sound therapy. I never want to be without it.''

Darrell Johnson, Box 615, Delisle, Sask., SOK OPE:

"About four years ago I started getting ringing in the left ear, followed by light-headedness and dizziness. Sometimes I couldn't stand without falling. This I was getting about once a month, then twice a month, soon twice a week and not long later three or four times a day. My doctor told me I had Meniere's Syndrome, which is a problem of the inner ear past the stirrup. There wasn't much that could be done; I would just have to put up with it. Being my age was 53, I knew I would be quite some time putting up with this problem. The doctor made some changes in my diet, which helped a little but not much. It was no cure, and I still got the spells. Then I heard about Sound Therapy. I bought the Sony Walkman and tapes on June 15/83. I played it three to five hours a day. It took about ten weeks before I noticed any difference. Now, four months later, I have no light-headedness and dizziness, and the ringing in my left ear has gone. Sometimes I get the feeling that I might get dizzy, and I put on the sound therapy music and the feeling goes away immediately. The hearing in my left ear has also improved. I can't express how much Sony and the tapes have done for me. I still use my Sony and tapes three to four hours a day, as it is so relaxing, and I am never dragged out and tired any more. I can stay up very late at night and still get up rested early in the morning. Also, I don't get uptight and stressed about the little setbacks of the day, but can just relax and take them in my stride.

I even find it easier to talk to people — am not so shy!
It's like a new life.''

Courtney Milne, photographer, Saskatoon:

"Since the Sound Therapy has taken effect for me,
I no longer know what anxiety is. As a photographer,
lecturer and writer, I am travelling continually and am
bombarded with more than average demands. Even at
the times of greatest pressure I feel an inner calm, a peace
and tranquility that lifts me above the stresses of the moment. I have no doubt at all that this is due to the therapy,
as I compare my present state with that of a year ago before I began the listening program. At that time I felt always harried, often exhausted and needed eight or nine
hours sleep a night; now five or six suffice, and I awake
deeply rested and with a supply of energy which remains
constant throughout my long days.

Although I experienced the opening of the ear some
months ago, I still listen for several hours daily, as I enjoy the music and it keeps my energy unflagging, my
peace intact. I find it extremely simple to wear my Walkman almost anywhere without it interfering. I drive, jog,
read, listen to the radio, carry on day-to-day conversations, eat my meals and do my photography while listening to the music. I would not be without it when writing
as it is conducive to creative thought, the music humming
along unobtrusively like a built-in mantra.

Sound Therapy also puts attention on caring for myself. It has had an influence on my eating and drinking

habits and my desire for regular exercise — a strengthening of the positive life wish. For example, as a moderate social drinker, it struck me one day that I have no need of alcohol to relax me or make me happy — so why drink any? I now jiggle my ice in a glass of fruit juice and no questions are asked . . . except the usual one: "Where do you get all that energy?"

Some brief comments from students at St. Peter's College, after a few months of listening to the cassettes on Sony Walkmans issued by the school:

Susan Stroeder: "I enjoyed this therapy and learned to pay more attention in school. I wake up easier in the morning — my Mom doesn't have to call me anymore. I don't have to ask questions twice, but hear things the first time."

Kyle Bauer: "I don't get headaches now and am much more active."

Marian Niekamp: "Don't need as much sleep and am not tired in the mornings. My speaking is much clearer."

Keith Carroll: "It made me much more calm and relaxed."

Lyle Witt: "My right ear seems to bug me when I listen to hard rock now."

Debbie Nagy: "I've been listening to the Walkman for over 600 hours. I find it very relaxing. I can sleep a lot better at nights. I wake up more easily in the mornings and find myself in better moods. I don't mind listening to it at school, and on weekends I try to get as many hours as I can. I find I can study a lot better and I'm more prepared for tests. I'm really enjoying the classical music."

And from Norman Altrogge, University student and part-time restaurant worker:

"Over and above assisting me in relaxing and winding down, my hearing became much keener as I listened to the cassettes from day to day. There followed improved concentration and it seemed easier to zero in on things. The listening had a sort of snowballing effect in improving my ability to focus my mind and put myself into whatever I'm doing with a larger degree of intensity."

Jeff Johnson, Graduate Student, Dept. of Humanities, S.U.N.Y., Buffalo:

"Not only has Sound Therapy enhanced my learning capabilities, but it has greatly increased my confidence in speaking. Being a graduate student means that you must be able to speak with authority to groups of highly intelligent people. In the past I have been too shy and self-doubting to give such presentations with any confidence. They were the most anxiety-provoking situations of my life. My hands used to shake and I would be wet with perspiration before beginning to speak. Not anymore. I carry my Sony Walkman and tapes in my briefcase, and for a time before speaking I immerse myself in the recharging sounds of the music. I find then that

I am perfectly at ease before large groups, and my presentations go without a hitch. Sound Therapy has helped me so much with my professional life that I've given it my own special name; I call it Confidence Therapy, because confidence was the area in which I was most lacking, and I now feel like a new man!"

Ed Rohner, President, United Fretters Ltd., Saskatoon:

"The greatest benefit that Sound Therapy has had for me so far is in the area of hearing. I have a noticeable improvement in hearing and need less volume on my Walkman all the time. Also, I'm aware of having acquired the capacity for more highs. Most important of all for a musician, I am getting closer to pitch. I find I'm able to compensate the tuning which is required on any string instrument. With the increase in musical perception I am getting much more critical of sound. I firmly believe that a person who was tone deaf would be able to change that condition with Sound Therapy."

Claude Heppell, Rimouski, Que.:

"The most recent effect of my Sound Therapy, after 14 months of listening to the tapes, is rather amusing: for I have lately discovered a capability of doing crosswords, at which I had slaved in vain in the past.

As a purely visual person, it took me a long time to realize effects with these tapes. I was patient and persistent, as I enjoyed the music and found that I missed it when I skipped a day. Gradually I found myself becoming a more social person, feeling more and more love for others, with a powerful new capacity to interact and create in volunteer groups for old people. I am 46, and whereas one might say this was a natural maturation, I believe that, on the contrary, change is more difficult as we get older.

A few months ago, singing some folksongs for my own pleasure, I realized I had more ability to strike the right notes than before. And when I speak, my voice, which I disliked until recently, is gradually becoming more resonant, warm, and well controlled. All thanks to the Sound Therapy cassettes and Walkman.''

Mrs. Helen Schatzley of Thompson, Manitoba:

''I used to take hours to get to sleep; now, ten minutes.

I do my husband's bookkeeping, often having to work whole days at it. Those days used to be very stressful . . . I had all sorts of upsets and made many mistakes. I now wear the headphones the entire time I'm working on the books and get through it like a breeze, with no mistakes.

The main effect of the Sound Therapy has been on my blood pressure. For years I had high blood pressure, 160/100 being an average level. After about two months listening to the cassettes with a Sony Walkman, my pressure began going down. One day during my check-up the nurse read my pressure and said, 'Wait a minute,

I'll have to get another machine, this one isn't working. There's no way your blood pressure is going to be 120/80.' But that's what it was.

Some months after that I went through a terrible time, caring for a demanding invalid, who called upon me day and night. I didn't put on the headphones during those weeks as I was afraid I might miss hearing her. (Now I know that crisis times are exactly when I should keep up the listening.) My blood pressure shot up to 225/127. After it was over I started listening to the music again and my pressure came down 50 points *in the first hour!* It soon returned to normal. My doctor was amazed. 'What have you been *doing?*' he asked. I showed him the book. He has now taken me off medication.

Not only that, but my hearing has improved tremendously. When I started the listening, I had to have the volume on my Walkman set at five or six . . . now I listen at a setting of one-half.

My husband is now doing the therapy and for starters has stopped snoring!''

Mrs. Schatzley sent a photograph of Dr. Schatzley and herself with their Walkmans and headphones — and a third family member, also wearing phones. She explains that their little cocker spaniel was hyperactive, and as the therapy has been so useful with hyperactive children, they decided to try the headphones on their dog. She says: "To our astonishment, the dog will sit and listen endlessly, remaining perfectly still. If we put any other music on her, she lifts her paw and knocks the headphones off.''

Others might find it merely amusing, and some traditionalists might scorn this use of the therapy; but a dog is endowed with inordinately sensitive hearing and suffers from harmful sounds as much or more than humans. This little cocker spaniel could be opening a door to a vast area of comfort and healing for animals of all kinds. They don't all have to wear headphones! Considering an animal's sensitivity, the music might be played softly over speakers in places where dogs are penned up in kennels, relieving their desperation and misery. Animal lovers can take it from there.

But it takes a dumb creature to know a beneficent sound when it hears one.

Judy and Gerrit Westerhof, Winnipeg:

"Our son John is in Grade 6 and showing terrific improvement in reading since beginning on the Sound Therapy tapes two months ago. He says a lot of people don't even know he is dyslexic anymore. His teachers are amazed and thrilled, and even his friends have noticed the change in him. John came home last week and reported that two boys said, 'Boy, John, you're a lot smarter this year. Last year you were so dumb, but this year you're not.' We are so excited, because last year John was in a special program and this year he is in the regular program. He was on medication for his learning disability, but is now off the Ritalin. It makes him especially happy that he doesn't have to take the pills anymore, as they made him sick to his stomach. He loves the baroque music, listening with his Auto-Reverse Walkman all night until the batteries run out. He hated to read before, and now when we have our evening devotions he asks to read and does it very well. It is like a miracle and he improves daily. His grandfather says it's like an alarm went off in his head and he woke up."

Carla Gaunt, a brain damaged, mentally handicapped teen-ager in Saskatoon, has been doing Sound Therapy for the past three months and loves listening to the tapes. Her parents report that there has been a great improvement in her ability to handle stress; her speech has developed and also her recall of past events.

Maureen Boyko, Watson, Sask.:

"Our son, Mitch, is going to St. Peter's Pre-Vocational Centre in Muenster. He has been listening to Sound Therapy tapes on an Auto-Reverse Walkman in school since he started there in Sept. of 84, and we've had them at home since our purchase in April 85, two months ago.

Sister Miriam, one of Mitch's teachers and also principal of the school, said she has noticed a real change in Mitch in the final two months of the school year. My husband and I have noticed a real difference as well. His posture has improved. He used to walk really slouched. We're not reminding him to stand straight nearly as often. He is more relaxed; he speaks out more clearly and more often. He used to speak so softly and did not articulate his words clearly. He feels that he has much better sleep, listening to the tapes. And last but not least he has developed a real appreciation of classical music."

Melanie King, singer-composer, Melbourne, Australia:

"I have had some beautiful benefits from using the tapes — trebled energy, less sleep needed, steadier moods, more focused concentration — and I have notes in the top of my vocal range which are brand new."

P.S., some months later: "My voice continues to soar eaglebound in new ways!"

Herbert Spanier, Toronto:

"My immersion into the world of Sound Therapy has had several positive results. A strikingly noticeable one was in my work as musical performer and composer, where my creative potential was dramatically opened up. The compliments I am receiving for my concerts, where improvisation is a key, are more numerous and enthusiastic, and this from contemporaries and audiences alike. Also in the areas of stress and fatigue, considerable modification is being observed."

Lorna Graham, Hardings Point, Clifton Royal, NB:

"I suffer from MS and have been listening to the Sound Therapy tapes for about three months. I have had great luck in stabilizing my energy and can carry on normally. Nothing else I have done has helped me the way the tapes have. The M stands for multiple or many, and so I need to do a lot of things, but the tapes really have helped bring it all together and make it worthwhile. They are a life saver to me. They also keep headaches at bay.''

Dr. Kathleen Langston, Naramata, B.C.

''After 16 years of almost constant phantom pain due to amputation of my right leg from a car accident, I feel I have now found an answer. When I got my Sony and tapes I had some response almost at once, and it kept getting better. I didn't really believe it would help when I started; I had used so many things for phantom pain, even self hypnosis, and had to take 292s 3 or 4 times a day. Now I rarely take them, and only for some other complaint. The good results continue. It truly seems like a miracle.''

Mrs. Gertrude Rempel Brown, Vancouver:

''It was pure accident that I heard Patricia Joudry being interviewed on radio. The word **tinnitus** caught my attention, and I began the Sound Therapy. My tinnitus, which my doctor said was incurable, **was cured** after several weeks of 3 hours a day listening. I had tinnitus for two years — and it was SHEER HEAVEN when it stopped — **not** to have incessant ringing in my ears. It also gives me a sense of well being. I am lending the book to my doctor!''

Dan Stuckel, Red Deer, Alberta:

"Before I began using the Sound Therapy tapes my hearing was becoming progressively worse. Ear specialists told me it was caused by nerve damage, therefore there was nothing which could be done for me. They said the ringing in my ears would become louder as time went on, thereby reducing my ability to hear. I purchased an 'in the ear model' hearing aid after I found their predictions to be correct. My hearing did indeed deteriorate. I found I had to wear the hearing aid more and more as time went on, to a point where I was wearing it 80% of the time.

After about 3 weeks of beginning the Sound Therapy, the ringing in my ears began to subside. Along with that my hearing also began to improve. One day I felt something almost like a minor earthquake taking place deep within my ears. Since then my hearing has improved to such an extent that I seldom have to use my hearing aid. I am able to function quite well without it now, after 7 months of Sound Therapy.

To list a few of the other benefits from this therapy: I am able to sleep better and can do with much less sleep than previously required. I am doing less needless worrying, and stressing situations are much easier to cope with than they were before. In fact my entire well being is showing a vast improvement."

James W. Bragg, Kentucky:

"Sound Therapy has transformed my life. I've been listening to the tapes for two months, and while I started feeling subtle effects almost immediately, the real change occurred about five weeks into the program.

To give a brief history: I have spent a lifetime surrounded by a good deal of noise, but always had sufficient energy until about 1972. I was building my house and using power saws and an assortment of very loud motorized tools. After less than a year of this, my energy level dropped to virtually nil — five minutes of work followed by thirty minutes of rest. It got progressively worse, and I was very worried. Loud sounds drove me frantic.

I teach piano at Morehead State University. Piano playing became extremely difficult for me. It got so I could hardly stand to do it. I have played publicly only three or four times since then, with three to five year rests between performances, and I was *never* satisfied with the results. It always seemed as if a short circuit existed in my expressive mechanism. I was aware of a lack of connection in the heart area and the parallel area in the spine, and worked very hard to *think* it together. Needless to say, it never worked.

Well, let me tell you! My sound has changed, and I *love* to play! The playing experience has been transformed. I seem to be hearing back the sound that I go for, and that affects the way I make the next sound. The musical cycle is now complete. With the experience of musical sounds being so greatly deepened and expanded, I am liking music which previously bored me and adoring music which I previously liked OK. The implications for the learning and teaching of music with this therapy are vast.

Then, for many years I have had great trouble with

my shoulders, upper spine and neck. It was never comfortable and the shoulders often painful in the extreme. Yoga made it worse. Activity hurt. I was a virtual cripple. I began to see a chiropractor, who said my upper spine was severely misaligned. During this period I began the Sound Therapy. At between five and eight weeks he was mystified to notice that the natural curvature of my spine was fully restored and assured me that he had not done it. He said he had never seen such a thing or heard of such a thing and would probably be drummed out of the profession if he wrote it up for a medical journal. My posture is transformed and I have real shoulders at last! This is obviously reflected in my playing since the shoulders are extremely important in piano playing.

In addition, I have had an elusive speech problem since childhood. Sometimes the speech was fluent and easy; other times it simply would not come out. I literally could not talk. Most people were not aware of it, since I 'cleverly' disguised my problem by acting 'professorial' — thinking a lot and talking very little and slowly. All of this had a devastating effect on my personality, creating mood swings which were violent and unexpected. Resultingly, depression became an old, old friend.

Now this is all changed. *I can talk!* Mood swings are very mild and no longer a problem. I truly feel that I am being myself for the first time in my life. I know who I am. Energy is greatly increased; stamina and endurance greatly improved. I sleep from two to four hours a night and awake feeling marvelous.

Just call me Lazarus!''

Chapter Seven

The Facts

This chapter is for people who would like the physiological facts about the ear and brain. We have treated rather light-heartedly a very serious and complex subject, partly because light-heartedness is of the essence of the effect itself, and also because to treat it with the seriousness and complexity it warrants would make it unreadable.

The important thing about this technique is to do it; that's all that matters. The baby who is crying and shuts off like a switch when the headphones are placed over its ears is the one who has the quickest response of all — except maybe the dog. The intellect is not required here, and in fact has been known to get in the way, for intellectuals tend to take longer than intuitives to open to the sound.

Therefore if you don't happen to be interested in the following facts, you should feel perfectly free to skip this chapter. For after reading it, though you may be smarter, you will be none the wiser.

The ear is the organ which helps the organism to adjust to its environment, but is not only a receptive organ with the character of intake. While the ear is a receiver from the environment, it also makes the choice as to what it will listen to from the total environment input. It is because of this that the ear gives origin to human consciousness. By means of its selective adjusting to the environment, the ear becomes the organ of adjustment to the environment.

The ear, of course, is a member organ of the total organism. The organism in its functioning as a complex system, and as an individual unity, which has to survive in the complex world, is orchestrated, controlled and guided by an ingenious Central Nervous System. The ear is a part of, and is an organ of the Central Nervous System.

The following pages present a few facts about the development and functional dynamics of this intricate master organ.

Brain and Language

The evolutionary history of mankind tells us that the human brain, which weighs only 1,400 grams, completed its biological development millions of years ago. This, however, was only the beginning of human development of the species which we see ourselves today. After the human brain attained this species-specific level of maturity, it did not stop evolving.

There is a saying that it is not known whether man

created language or the language made man. It is a fact that mankind's superiority among other living beings is intrinsically related to the language development as a vehicle for human thought processes and for a creative approach in the struggle for survival.

The human brain, as the rest of the organism, originated from one fertilized cell. However, in just two to four weeks from the moment of conception, the neural tube is already detectable in the embryo. It is the first of the organ systems to leap ahead along Nature's preprogrammed plan. After several regular divisions the neuronal cells begin growing their axons and dendrites. These primitive cells do not divide or increase in numbers. The dendritic proliferation initially is determined by internal factors; at later stages it is influenced and stimulated by surrounding tissues and stimulation from the maternal environment.

At birth the infant's brain is already highly developed. However, the complexity of neuronal connectivities is far from being complete. It is through heredity that the brain is received, but it take many years after birth — the ontogenesis — before the person becomes an independent, self-conscious and creative member of our society. To achieve this goal, Nature pre-arranged to leave the human brain in a state of resiliency and plasticity. It is the nurturance, the process of acculturation that patterns and shapes the brain. Language, in its spoken and written form, is the vehicle of cultural transmission.

The brain is predisposed for speech from before birth. The speech areas in the cortex — the left planum temporale — is larger in 65 per cent of human brains in utero. The left temporal hemisphere is found to be a speech/language seat in 95 per cent of the population by the age of four or five.

Predisposition for language is biological. The organs and organ systems, including those involved in language functions, are species specific, hence human. The messages that language carries are due to acculturation, societal membership and personal development.

The Brain

The brain is to be viewed as a complex system composed of well-identifiable anatomical units, its macrostructure: namely two cerebral hemispheres linked by a great commisural structure, the corpus calosum. The hemispheres are connected by crisscrossing nerve fibers vertically, downward, with the lower levels of the brain. Diencephalon, thalamus and basal ganglia, via millions of nerve fibers, link the cerebral hemispheres, neocephalon, with still lower levels of mesencephalon. The mesencephalon is composed of the pons, the cerebellum, the medulla, and the spinal cord.

This vertical downward view of the brain must be kept in mind to enable us to understand that the messages, through sense organs from the outside world, as well as the messages from within the body, must be linked. The messages from outside have to be integrated with the needs of the organism, and the needs of the organism must be recognized to make the outside world desirable or meaningful to the individual. In fact, the cerebral cortex is the receiver and analyzer of all the information that reaches the senses, but the motivating search for information flows from below upwards. The cortex then has a manifold task: first, to register the flow of information; then in "consultation" with the visceral and emotional brain (diencephalon), it has to weigh the value of sensory input, and only in view of that to organize the appropriate action strategies to carry out the response.

If the outline of the brain appears complex in its constituent parts, so much more intricate are the microstructures of it. Lots of unresolved problems for neuroscientists still remain to be unravelled. What is already known is very mysterious. The neocortex, for example, is only three mm thick, but contains about 10,000 million neurons! Electron microscopy reveals that these millions of neurons are not packed as a mass, but each one is separated from the others by its enveloping membrane. When a neuron is excited it transmits impulses in the form of a brief electrical wave. These impluses travel in an all-or-nothing manner along all nerve fibers at high velocities. Each neuron has hundreds or even thousands of connecting points with other neurons called synapses. As an illustration: the connection of the cerebral cortex with lower levels of the brain, the corpus calosum, has about two million connecting fibers.

With so many neurons and such a network of connectedness there must be some system, some order to make sense of neuronal firings. The neuroscientists suggest that the neocortex should be viewed as a mosaic of discrete units or modules. The modules are like "power units" of the brain. They are distributed at different levels of architechtonics of the cortex and interconnect via the neuronal pathways between primary sensory inputs with the secondary and tertiary sensory areas horizontally. At the same time the messages flow to and are received from secondary and tertiary areas. The thalamus becomes a liaison or exchange station, and reticular formations of the brain stem maintain the state of vigilance.

Millions of neurons, each having hundreds of thousands of connecting tracks, through each of these high velocity firings could indeed blow the brain. Fortunately, Nature is wiser than that. The power units or modules of the brain have some of these units excitatory, while others are inhibitory. Thus, nowhere is there uncontrolled excitation. As yet there is no computer which can equal the dynamic functionality of the brain: about 4 million modules each with about 2,500 component neurons, all working in harmony.

From Neurons to Perception

The glimpse of complexities of the brain tells us about the great living factory which receives the impulses of physical energy and enables the human being (perhaps some animals in a similar way) to perceive. This means that by means of our brain we see colours, shapes; we hear sounds; we feel hunger, pain, pleasure, etc. The cortex, within the mosaic of millions of its modules, divides the task to do the job of transformation of electric impulses into perception. The cortex is specialized for analysis of different inputs and in organization of action systems for reaction. Each of the specialized areas receives the energy potential in so-called primary areas and horizontally spreads it to the secondary and tertiary areas. While the sensory stimuli propagate to the primary areas of the cortex, the brain stem is already alerted. In the process of associative elaboration of the input in the secondary and the tertiary cortical areas the feedbacks involve the thalamic integrative network. At the time the perceiver derives an image, a representation of reality, the sensory information becomes imbued with emotional feeling. There is no such thing as an "objective" perception. All perceptual contents have imprints of emotional, subjective experience.

It is in this context that the notion of plasticity of the brain becomes relevant. The neuronal dendrification and connectivity of modules with their intricate connections is stimulated by the sensory inputs. It is known that through hypnosis or self-hypnosis, such as yogic exercises, an individual is able to inhibit afferent inputs or sensory excitation, and reduce or even eliminate feeling, i.e., perception of pain. In the same way a person can render more acute sensitivity to certain stimuli by tuning down the competing stimulation. A younger individual, particularly an infant or a child, who is much more alert to bodily needs, may turn away from outside stimuli that have the flavour of unpleasantness. This way, while avoiding frustration, he also is cutting himself off from necessary sensory stimulation. In clinical experience there are known cases of sensory deprivation due to lack of nurturance. In such cases there will be partial/specific or total lack of neuronal development.

The neuroscientists also suggest that the lack of sustained sensory inputs may cause failures of long-term memory. Short-term memory is explained as a result of cortical activity on the level of associative, horizontal connections. Long-term memory calls for increased efficiency of neuronal connectedness. A sensory input event has to be repeated from three minutes to three hours. Attention and concentration have to be sustained. Subcortical units, hippocampus (diencephalon) and cerebellar activity have to be registered. The neocortex has the task of recording not only the information, perceptual givens, but also the involvement of action systems, perception of self or proprioceptorial input. Long-term memory, thus, records events on a conscious level, intentionally and willfully.

The Ear

The ear is a highly specialized organ. It is complex, and in its functionality it reveals its interconnectedness with the total organism. Its main function is to help an individual — a human as well as an animal — to adjust to its living space, the environment.

Dr. Tomatis stresses the acquaintance with embryological foundations of the ear because the embryology of the ear explains the mechanisms of the auditory apparatus.

The anatomical structures composing the ear are: external ear (the penna), the meatus (external canal), tympanic membrane, three ossicles of the middle ear (hammer, anvil, stirrup), and the cochlea or the inner ear.

Although the semicircular canals are not viewed as organs of hearing, it is difficult to bypass their direct connection with the inner ear. The connection between the inner ear and semicircular canals is smoothed out by two pocketlike sacs (sacculum and utriculum). The cochlea, the connecting sacs and semicircular canals are filled with endolymphatic liquid.

From the tympanus on, the ear is encased in a porous mastoid bone. The only opening to the outside besides the external ear canal is the Eustachian tube. It connects the middle ear cavity with the mouth, and serves the purpose of maintaining constant pressure upon the tympanic membrane. The pressure tension of the inner ear is regulated by the resiliency of the membranes of the two windows, the oval and the round, both of which are located within the bone containing the cochlea.

Embryologically, as soon as the embryo begins to differentiate into organs, there is an indication of common origin between the maxillary bone (inferior mandibule) and the two ossicles of the middle ear, the hammer and the anvil. Since, to be functional, the bones need musculature, the muscles that control the mandibule and the two ossicles, hammer and anvil, come from the same mesodermal embryonic structure. Furthermore, the muscles are activated by the same pair of cranial nerves, the Vth pair or trigeminal. The stirrup instead, the third of the middle ear ossicles, originates from the same tissue as the upper part of the larynx, the hyoid bone. To the hyoid bone are attached the muscles controlling the tongue and the digastric muscle. This muscle serves to open the mouth. It also controls the musculature of the face, except the muscles which control the eyelids. All the above musculature is activated by the VIIth pair of cranial nerves (the facial nerve).

The ear is lined with the same tissue as the mouth. The inner ear is a space, hence an organ for ingestion.

The ear, which is traditionally viewed as being divided into three parts, external, middle and internal, should, according to Dr. Tomatis, be viewed as composed only of two parts: external and internal. The dividing line, due to different embryonic origins and different neuronal connections, is at the level of the anvil and the stirrup. The hammer and the anvil belong to the external portion; the stirrup to the portion of the inner ear. In terms of functions, the external ear is vital in sensory input. The internal ear, comprising the stirrup, is the organ of analysis and of perceptual accommodation.

Only the above delineated embryologically diverse origin of the outer ear and inner ear allows the inference that functionally these structures carry different assignments.

To perform a function or service to the organism the organ has to "know" its master. The IXth and Xth pairs of the cranial nerves accomplish this task. The Xth pair or the vagus is a visceral nerve par excellence, which is also a "watchdog." It sits at the gates of the external ear and also has a vested interest in the mechanism of phonation. The IXth pair interacts with the vagus nerve at the level of the pharynx and transfers messages collected from the vagus to the spinal column. Both of these nerves are called glossopharyngial, which means that they are entrusted with the controls of the phonatory apparatus. The vagus informs us about visceral needs; the IXth nerve determines our posture.

This brief embryological overview stresses the fact that the ear, including the auditory nerve, the VIIIth pair of cranial nerves, develops from the germinal plasma topographically very close to the pneumogastric nerve, the vagus. The ear is an organ to serve the organism. It has therefore to be informed as much about what is occurring in the organism as about what the environment offers to its needs.

The Inner Ear

For non-professionals the ear is what we see externally. Most ear or hearing difficulties are viewed as middle ear problems, ear infections. The external ear is important since it is an organ of sensory intake. However, the essential organ of hearing is deeply hidden and highly protected within the bone. It is, in fact, very difficult to penetrate into it even for the scientist. Until very recently most substantial research on how our mind transforms brain work into knowledge of the environment has been done by the study of vision.

It has been long understood that within the cochlea are contained specialized nervous cells, Corti cells. These are distributed over the basilar membrane along the cochlear snail, about 30 or so millimetres in length. Corti cells recall aquatic microorganisms; they each have 50 to 100 cilia. They are seated on supportive cells and are arranged in two layers: 3,500 cells are more internal, 21,000 of them are more external. The distribution along the basilar membrane is not homogeneous. More cells are at the base, closer to the stirrup. As the cochlear space is restricted toward the distal end, there is less space to accommodate the precious cellular material.

The ciliate Corti cells are covered with membranous tissue, the tectorial membrane. Consequently the cells are contained between two membranes and immersed in corti-lymph, while the cochlear labyrinth is perilymphatic.

Whatever input comes into the inner ear is transmitted to the auditory cortex (temporal lobe) via the VIIIth pair of auditory nerves. As suggested the cortex not only receives, but checks, organizes and sends messages back to the sensory organs. The eye receives the light and colour carriers in the form of different electromagnetic waves; the brain accommodates the eyes via oculomotor nerves to look at, to explore, and so finalizes the perception of objective world facts. The same applies to the ear. The sound wave reaches the cochlea. It gathers information and, via the auditory nerve, transmits it to the cortex. The same auditory nerve brings back to the inner ear impulses from the brain, enriched and corrected by the total brain's input. In view of "insights" from the brain the ear listens to, explores, and scrutinizes the source of information. It is not the eye or the ear, but the "I" which centers the gaze and tends the ear to accomplish the task.

To accomplish a goal-directed act of listening the control of posture, the alerted state of the organism, is needed. This has also been prearranged. The inner ear works in total harmony with the vestibular system, the main duty of which is control of posture and tonicity. The auditory nerve acts in synergy of the cochlear and vestibular branches of the VIIIth pair of cranial nerves. Along the road from the ear to the brain the two branches of the auditory nerve make their contacts and exchanges of information passing several networks. The vestibular nerve, for example, enters into contact with oculomotor nerves, IIIrd, IVth and VIth pairs. It is for this reason that while we listen we also turn our gaze in that direction; if we wear eyeglasses we reach for them when we concentrate on listening.

The Functional Dynamics of the Inner Ear

What is the sensory material the ear is dealing with? The answer that comes to mind is sound. But it is not sound; it is only input of energy due to the bombardment of air particles. If we were in a closed tube from which all the air was absorbed, we not only could not breathe, we could not hear either. The air bombards or caresses not only the ear but all of the body. We, in fact, hear throughout all of our body, skin, tissues, and in particular through our bones. It is the same as with light. All the body is caressed by the sun. The skin can pick up, however, only the warmth, while the eye is selectively picking out the rays of light. The ear in the same way picks out the range of vibrations which caresses the body, but is preprogrammed to select only a certain range of wave lengths of air movements. This range of wavelengths is from 16 cycles per second to about 16,000 cycles per second.

The long waves are interpreted as rumours or noises. The range between 300 cycles per second and 3,000 cycles per second carries the human voice. To this stimulation the human ear is also most sensitive. In Nature's plan the human voice and the ear are in a relationship of interdependency. In the human the lungs, larynx, pharynx and mouth produce the vibrations of air; the ear captures the vibrations, controls the phonatory apparatus, and modulates the voice. Only the human child discovers that he can produce complex sounds at will. It is long known that to be able to speak one has to hear. Before one hears the other, the model for a given language idiom, he has to become aware of and master his auditory apparatus and appreciate the tiny trickles of air that flow out of his own respiratory system.

In so-called classical theories of hearing it is assumed that "sound waves reach the external ear, penetrate through the meatus, vibrate its tympanic membrane, and thus engage the chain of the middle ear ossicles (the hammer, anvil and stirrup) into movement. Through these media the wave reaches the cavity of the internal ear. In the internal ear, the transmission of the sound wave by displacement of the base of the stirrup at the oval window induces the movement of the endolymphatic liquid according to the frequency range and stimulates the Corti cells which are distributed on the basilar membrane."[1]

Such an interpretation of events that take place in the process of hearing is only partial. It does not accom-

---

[1]Revue Internationale d'Audiopsychophonologie, p. 46.

modate the dynamics of feedbacks from the brain. It may be acceptable, therefore, as an explanation of sensory intake but in no way does it explain the function of the ear as a perceptual organ.

Dr. Tomatis' explanation of the ear's role takes into account the sensory as well as perceptual, hence psychological task that the ear has to perform.

First of all, Dr. Tomatis calls attention to the communality between the vestibular apparatus and the cochlea. Both of these organs have maintained their liquidian milieu. The endolymph is not only responsive to the body's mass movements, such as movements of the head, but also to the subtle movements of maintaining posture: antigravitational or equilibrium movements. The utriculum controls horizontality, the sacculum — verticality; the semicircular canals register the directionality of movements and, through the interplay of the movements of a liquid mass in a closed space, engender a sense of timing, hence perception of rhythm. Since activation of the vestibular reaches the brain stem and the spinal cord, it induces the perception of proprioceptivity. It is easy to see the movement of the body as a cause of endolymphatic vibrations; it is more difficult to view the liquidian mass as if it were a "living" medium that is in constant excitement. Not only the mass but also the molecular particles are at all times in activity. It is this activity, and not only the vibrations induced by external inputs, that is to be considered as stimuli evoking proprioceptorial sensations.

What goes on in vestibular canals and in particular

in their bridges with the cochlea — utriculum and sacculum — occurs also in the cochlea. While vestibular communications of its activities remain unconscious, the cochlea, instead, has the assignment of analyzing the inputs on the cortical level and transforming them into perceptions. The inner ear picks up the vibrations of the liquidian mass movements as well as molecular excitations of the endolymph and of the whole labyrinthine milieu in which it is encased.

The basilar membrane, over which are inserted Corti cells upon the supportive or "container" cells, is, in fact, a continuation of the bony spiral. The vibrations or molecular excitations from the bony spiral spread to the tectorial membrane, the cover sheet over the Corti cells. Whatever affects the bony labyrinth, in which the cochlea is placed, makes the total cochlear mass and its molecular structure vibrate. The excitation that is in the inner ear is always an internal input; all external inputs penetrating the ear are transformed into vibrations of the inner ear's own substance.

Any musical instrument produces sound by all its body. The body material and the encased air mass in it vibrate in its finest molecular particles. The cochlea is such an instrument. It responds in its totality to the bony structures of the labyrinth and spiral as well as to its liquidian contents which vibrate within their most subtle constituents.

The Ear as a Functional Organ

As in a musical instrument the cochlear labyrinth vibrates as an oscilator, the vesicle as a resonator. The cochlear labyrinth responds to all vibrations that touch upon it. It is the task of the ear as a whole, as an organ in service to the organism, to sort out what to respond to, i.e. how to select what to listen to. The bones of the skull, the bony structure of the labyrinth, the aquaducts, the antechambers between the vestibular canals and cochlea, utriculum and sacculum, the two windows, the round and the oval, the middle ear ossicles up to the pavilion of the external ear, are the functional accessories to protect the very highly sensitive organ which is the inner ear.

The bony structures transform the physical energy of external sources from the mass movements to molecular excitement. However, if and when sudden and very strong movements bypass the first controls the cochlear liquidian contents have a valve releasing the pressure, the round window. If the turbulence affects the endolymph on the side of the vestibular canals the turbulence is relieved by spreading into the sacculum and exerting pressure upon the oval window.

The oval window is closed by the base of the stirrup and controlled by musculature. The oval window, in Dr. Tomatis' conception of the dynamics of hearing, is totally different from the round window. The oval window which closes and opens on an axle like a piston acts under efferent stimulation, i.e. under cortical control. The stapedius or the plate of the stirrup controls strong vibrations particularly coming from the articulatory apparatus.

These bodily noises via direct bone conduction if not controlled would drown all other information provenient from the outside world. The stirrup thus deadens the inner bodily noises to enable us to hear, to analyze or perceive the information essential for adaptation. It is common to people who start losing their hearing to be afflicted by inner, bodily rumours and sizzling sounds. This happens when the stapedius loses its functionality and the ear its purposefulness.

The movement of the stapedial plate of the stirrup also serves to assess the sensation of the intensity of outside inputs. As any other organ, it has its functional limits. When the pressures exceed normal limits for stapedial movement the whole body reflects discomfort; a person becomes rigid and irritable. This indicates that postural and proprioceptorial sensations reflect difficulties on the level of the inner ear. The high intensity sounds may also affect the Corti cells. Scotomas always occur in the most vulnerable spot of the cochlear reception organ (4,000 Hz). Whether the sounds are high or low frequency, under high intensity they hit the vulnerable area of the tectorial membrane. This is the area with the thickest concentration of Corti cells.

Where the stirrup and its stapedial plate control inner bodily noises, the tympanus is the receiver of the outer inputs. Its tension is controlled by the hammer and anvil. The tympanus is the first station where the external source is transformed into a form of energy compatible with the inner ear's requirements. In this process the mid ear ossicles are not used in a mechanical way. While there is some movement of the total mass of the tympanus the sound energy is absorbed by the membrane and transmit ted in a molecular form via bones to the vesicle of the inner ear.

The tympanus is controlled by the hammer-anvil in degrees of tenseness as well as positioning. The tympanic membrane is not a mechanical obstacle in the way of the incoming stimuli. It is the organ which serves the organism. It is therefore under the control of the organism, of the brain, and of the mind. Since the essential organ for the analysis of sound is the inner ear, it is the inner ear, through the stirrup, that controls the tympanus disposing it to listening or becoming passive, relaxed. It is true that the ear is always open. Sound penetrates the organism on the unconscious level. However, as soon as consciousness is alerted, man tends his ears, and either listens to and accepts the message or turns away. As the eye is regulated automatically to the intensity of light, to the point of even closing the eyelids, so the ear, even without conscious effort, makes its adjustments. As the eye has to be directed to look intentionally so the ear is accommodated to listening by the working brain from within.

The pavilion or penna of the external ear and the ear canal already eliminate the very low frequencies and accommodate the flow-in of the waves between 800 Hz to about 4,000 Hz. Intuitively, to hear faint and distant sounds, we tend to touch by hand the pavilion of the ear and push it forward. The ear pavilion as well as the horizontally opposite positions of two ears, help in the localization of the origin of sound.

The ear canal has a twofold role. It serves as a filter. Its physical dimensions dictate its range. The incoming wave, like in a wind instrument, has to blend with the vibratory harmonics characteristic to the container. The canal also serves as the passage of "security." The Vth, VIIth and Xth pairs of cranial nerves spread within the skin of the canal passages do not remain inert. The Vth and the VIIth pairs alert the two gates of the ear, the tympanus and the stirrup; the Xth pair, or vagus, informs the vital organs. Before the auditory stimulus reaches the interior of the cochlea, it already is detected; it may therefore penetrate the organism as a welcome guest or as an intruder . . . to whom the gates may be closed. . . .

Body Image

All matter vibrates. All vibrations can be transformed into sound if they are captured by consciousness. To reach consciousness the complex sensory organ of audition is needed.

The lower species of the aquatic milieu apparently did not need the ear for this task. What was phylogenetically an organ of touch and kinesthesias for the aquatic animals, such as a lateral line in the fish, is today the auditory system for both animals and humans. As the evolutionary progression moved forward and living creatures reached the shores of dry land, the vestibular apparatus evolved. The vestibular branch of the auditory nerve is therefore the precursor of the auditory system. It controls sensory intake, mobility and posture by capturing vibrational impulses in the liquid-filled vestibular canals and their antechambers (utriculum and sacculum). The vestibular system was sufficient to the animal world. Their sound, which some scientists call communication, is in fact reflex-controlled emission of species-specific calls dictated by organismic needs. In some species of birds and aquatic mammals, such as whales and dolphins, the range of communication is enriched by melodies imprinted at the early stages of their brain development. This perfecting of the auditory apparatus goes hand in hand with the appearance of the cochlear precursor, the lagaena. The acquisition of the cochlea means cephalization, or awareness of and transformation of vibrations into perception of sound.

Humans, while evolving in the complexity of the nervous system and the refinement of the sensory organs, have retained the same sensitivities of touch, movement, and postural controls common to the other living species. People register air vibrations with the total body, as do animals. In fact, because of the vertical position humans are much more exposed to their environment. The skin is a sensory organ. It comes from the same embryonic layer as the rest of the nervous system. The vestibular apparatus in humans registers all the vibrations due to external movements as well as to the imperceptible vibrations flowing form within the organism. What makes human beings different from animals is the gift of the cochlea. By cochlear transmissions of sensations to the brain and by brain-mind feedbacks, the cochlea creates the image of humankind.

Homunculus

The homunculus concept was re-introduced into the neurosciences by Penfield, a neurosurgeon, not as an accomplished little man in the brain or pineal gland to take the place of the mind or soul, but as a representation of the body on the sensory and motor areas of the brain. As external senses the eye and the ear have specialized localizations in the cortex; so the inputs from the organs themselves register their presence of touch or movement in the sensory areas on the parietal lobe. When the brain sends messages, the organization of efferent or motor impulses is controlled by the motor cortex. So there are two homunculi on the cortex to represent proprioceptorial inputs and motor behaviours.

Iridologists can read bodily functioning from the iris of the eye. Dr. Tomatis proposes that audiologists ought to read the same into the ear's functions. He views the inner ear along the basilar membrane as a homunculus or a topographic representation of the total body.

We know that the inner ear transforms the sensations of the organism into a conscious Body Image or the Self. The inner ear however has another and more critical task, namely the analysis of input from the environment.

To accomplish this task the ear acts as a system: the external and inner ear structurally and functionally fit each other. Namely, the pavilion of the ear (or penna) is inervated in front by trigeminal (Vth pair) and at the back by facial (VIIth pair) nerves. These two pairs of nerves control the main gateways to the ear. The trigeminal controls the tympanus (the eardrum); the facial controls the stirrup with its stapedial plate at the oval window. However, as the stimuli reach the external ear, the total organ is alerted.

By anatomical structure the external ear is preprogrammed to receive wavelengths from 800 to 4,000 Hz. The cochlea deals with intensity (loudness), tonicity (pitch), harmonics (timbre), and semantics (language).

The ear is always alert; the Corti cells are always active. It maintains equilibrium between organismic inputs and the environmental sound background. Whenever a specific stimulus or wave pattern carrying a message reaches the ear the organism as a whole is alerted. The ear becomes a listening organ.

If the incoming sound is too intense defenses are set up. The tympanus tenses up, the inner ear is alerted, the stirrup opens the oval window and via the anvil and hammer releases tympanic tension. The tympanus relaxes and the incoming stimuli are blocked. At the same time the mouth opens, equalizing the pressure of the middle ear cavity in correspondence with the outside stimulation.

In all of this procedure the bone transmits to the liquidian milieu of the inner ear vibrations creating turbulence. Within the inner ear the tectorial membrane excites the Corti cells via its cilia. If the intensity, particularly of low frequency sounds, is too great, the basilar membrane may be damaged by the sound's penetration into it via the bony spiral and may be damaged by it. If the high frequency sounds are too intense the shock affects the cilia of the Corti cells and is registered as a sensation of pain.

Acupuncturists have localized the points in the skin surface of the pavilion of the ear, which have correspondence to all the internal organs. If the appropriate points in the external lobe of the ear are stimulated, then the corresponding organ is stimulated and energized. The sensitivity of the external ear in no way exceeds the analytical and discriminating functionality of the inner ear, the cochlea.

To assess cochlear responses to sound patterns an audiometer is used. The audiometer's range of frequency is in the range of 125 to 8,000 frequencies. The ear is most sensitive to the frequency range characterizing the human voice. In the normal ear this sensitivity increases six to 18 decibels per octave between 500 and 2,000 Hz. It reaches its highest peak at 2,000 and 4,000 Hz and then has a slight decline.

In audiometric practice the hearing tracing is represented as linear. To obtain a straight line on the audiometric tracing the low and high frequency inputs have been boosted in intensity and the audibility curve by mathematical calculations was straightened. Dr. Tomatis, however, insists that despite these corrections, camouflage of the sensitivity of the inner ear is not complete. In a musically sensitive ear the preferential zone between 1,000 and 2,000 Hz still stands out.

An audiometrician views his measurements as indicators of a normal or pathological sensory input, hearing. Dr. Tomatis' grasp and presentation of the auditory system as a perceptual organ opposes this reductionistic approach. He then proposes that audiometric testing and consequently the tracings obtained should be interpreted as listening attitudes as well as hearing thresholds.

Like every organ, the auditory system in a living organism is affected by life's experiences. Exposures to environmental sounds, if threatening, elicit the organism's defense mechanisms. These in time become stagnated in positions either of exclusion of sounds by the locked-in control system of the external ear, or overly tensed positions of overalertedness of the cochlea. These may be too intense environmental noises, low or high in pitch, or psychological hurts conditioning the defenseless child to turn away from some contacts.

As do audiometricians so audio-psycho-phonologists, following Dr. Tomatis' guidelines, administer the listening test via air and bone conduction. Dr. Tomatis stresses the fact that all transmission, be it captured by the external ear or directly reaching the inner ear from within the organism, is transmitted to the cochlea through the bone. However, the tracings obtained via air and bone conduction differ. In the air conduction the cochlea selectively receives information from the outside world; the bone conduction transmits the vibrations flowing via tissues and bones directly to the inner ear. The two tracings therefore reflect the concordance or divergence between listening and self-listening. The reading of tracings becomes a projective test; it indicates how one feels in the surrounding world as well as within. In a well-adjusted individual the two tracings are congruent.

As language is seated in the left hemisphere's temporal lobe, so the right ear (due to the crossed pathways of the corpus calosum) becomes the leading ear in the interpretation of the flow of language and of the processing of thought.

Sound Therapy a la Tomatis

The study of the ear as a functionally integrated complex system led Dr. Tomatis to the concept of audio-psycho-phonology. In other words, he explained the cybernetics of the audiovocal apparatus. He summarized the theory and data of experimentation in the laws that bear the Tomatis Effect name. This information is drawn from Andre Le Gall.

The first and most fundamental law is: "The voice contains only what the ear hears." The same law can be paraphrased also in terms of a vocal apparatus: "The larynx only emits the harmonics which the ear can hear." In terms of more technical rendition it can be said that there is "an exact and total correspondence for all frequencies shown on the audiogram and phonogram of the sounds heard and the sounds emitted."

The second law of Tomatis, which is the corollary to the first, states: "If the possibility of correctly hearing the frequencies that are lost or compromised is restored to the injured ear, these frequencies are instantaneously and unconsciously restored in the vocal emission."

The third law is presented by Andre Le Gall in Longchambon's wording: "Hearing which is compulsory, continual and repeated over a certain period of time definitely modifies hearing and speech."

The second and the third laws suggest that audio-psycho-phonatory therapy is possible whenever the disturbance of speech or voice are of psychological origin. Lack of training or faulty approach to communication can be corrected by Sound Therapy.

The organism is a resounding instrument. In cases of organovegetal and intestinal troubles the first to suffer is the voice. Visceral disturbances close the glottal passages, and preclude the voice emission. The voice has a "congested" tonal quality. The listening test shows a loss of "hearing" above 2,000 Hz. Individuals, children and adults alike, afflicted by such a disorder are apathetic, irritable and hypochondriac. Sound Therapy, i.e. stimulation of the ear by listening to pre-arranged tapes with bands of frequencies below 2,000 Hz filtered out, re-animates the organism. This effect can be understood if we remember that the inner ear is connected with the vestibular systems. Tonicity and posture are awakened and by experiential neuronal imbeddedness at the thalamus level, connections with inputs of vegetative needs and emotionality are engaged.

The most astounding effect of Sound Therapy occurs, in fact, in regulations of mood and vigilance; manic agitation and anxiety and depression are always reflected in the voice. Singers have described how their emotional states either hamper or help them in stage performances. In the flow of speech as well as in singing, the musculature of the phonatory apparatus is controlled by the motor and frontal cortical areas. These in turn are in a tight communication with the limbic lobes (the center of emotions) as well as with all the complexities of the diencephalon.

The phonatory apparatus may succumb to the unconscious inhibitions engendering an anxiety state. The performer acting upon his conscious and intentional command of the audiophonatory system is being broken down by dissociation from his bodily self. Sound Therapy reconciles the bodily and conscious self through the ear's all embracing regulatory influence.

Sleeplessness is also a symptom of lack of integration between the unconscious bodily self and the conscious and goal-directed, confident one. This process of dissociation fires neuronal excitations and overpowers cortical analysis. The reconciliation of the conscious and unconscious flow of information via harmonious working of the ear through Sound Therapy, clears sleeplessness.

Apathy, laziness and sleepiness are signs of a torpid condition of the total nervous system. The ear, stimulated by sound due to its all pervasive reach of bodily systems, awakens the mind.

The stutterer who seems unable to give commands to the articulatory organs must be reminded that it is the ear that is the master of the body. The stammerer has to re-train the leading (right) ear, and listen to his or her own voice before forcing an articulated word. The Electronic Ear of Dr. Tomatis has helped many of these people to discover self-listening as a condition "sine qua non" for articulation of the spoken word.

Many people, on first hearing how much is promised to those who undertake Sound Therapy according to Tomatis' method, shake their heads. To those who submit themselves in a spirit of faith the effects of the therapy confirm the promise. Those who are hesitant or frightened to try something so new, should consider these facts. Knowing how the nervous system works, and how the auditory system mediates between bodily needs and the world outside makes it easier to accept sound as a tonic, as a harmonizing agent of our own turbulence.

References

This chapter is prepared on the information contained in the following books:

1. Hess, W. R., **The Biology of the Mind,** the University of Chicago Press, 1964.

2. Eccles, John C., **The Human Mystery,** the Gifford Lectures University of Edinburgh, 1977-78.

3. Penfield, Wilder, **The Mystery of the Mind, a Critical Study of Consciousness and the Human Brain,** Princeton University Press, 1975.

4. Tomatis, A. A., **Vers l'Ecoute Humaine,** les editions ESF, Paris, 1974, Volumes 1 and 2.

Mimeographed materials.

5. Le Gall, Andre, **The Adjustment of Certain Psychological and Psycho-Pedagogical Deficiencies with Tomatis Effect Apparatus.**

6. **Introduction to the Listening Test,** Observations made during the third International Congress of Audio-Psycho-Phonology (Auver, 1973), in a question-and-answer session with Dr. A. A. Tomatis.

7. **Language,** the ideas of Dr. A. A. Tomatis as presented by A. E. Sidlauskas, Revue Internationale d'Audiopsychophonologie, 1974.

Tape information and prices on last page.

Appendix

Further Reports From Sound Therapy Listeners

Dorothy Hoag, Victoria, B.C.

"I am 78, and I used to have serious migraine headaches, about twice a month. In the 3 months since beginning Sound Therapy, I have not had a migraine or any kind of headache. It is wonderful to feel so good — relaxed — and sleep much better too. But the best thing, which I didn't anticipate, has been the improvement in hearing. For a long time my ears had some sort of pressure inside — like a bubble pressing on both sides — and this affected my hearing. The ear specialist looked at me as if I was out of my mind when I told him about the bubbles, and had no idea what it was. After hearing tests he said I would be "looking at a hearing aid" in a few years. But I am not going to be looking at that hearing aid! Through Sound Therapy the bubbles are gone and my hearing is improving steadily. I listen usually about five hours a day and do my work in house and garden listening to my tapes. They are great!"

Two years later. Dorothy Hoag reports: "I still listen several hours a day and the migraine headaches have never returned. Nor do I have any further trouble with my ears. Also my doctor says my blood pressure is *perfect*."

Dr. J. L. Koch, Mt. Vernon, Ohio:

"I felt I should not get too excited about the therapy until a fair amount of time had elapsed. I am now in my sixth month of the listening, and have never neglected the three to five hours spent as required for the best result. I celebrated my 77th birthday in September, and will admit to having more energy at 77 than I did at 67. All the benefits mentioned in your book have happened, with special reference to improvement in hearing."

Elsie Edson, 150 Mile House, B.C.

"I have been doing the therapy for approximately six weeks. The effect on my frazzled nerves has been dramatic, in a natural, subtle way. My thinking is clear and I have a strong sense of well being. I love the "hiss" of the electronic ear. It seems to penetrate deeper than the music. I believe it has been instrumental in relieving me of migraine headaches. Most of all, I am more relaxed and able to enjoy life more fully. Thus I am more pleasant to be around and also am able to have a more calming effect on others I come in contact with."

Mary Johnson, Bellevue, Washington:

"After a few months' listening I have really noticed a tolerance to high pitched sound — on radio, work place, etc. I used to turn our car radio on to bass because the treble irritated my ears. Now have no problem there."

Lorna Cooley, Victoria, B.C.

"My husband suffered for many years with very bad headaches, which sometimes lasted for several days. Since receiving our tapes four months ago, we have each averaged more than 4 hours a day of listening. Since the first week or two my husband has not had any more of those headaches. It has also helped me, by lowering my blood pressure and giving me much more energy. My husband is 75 and I am 73. Your Sound Therapy sure is a gift for us older people, as well as the younger ones."

Valerian Muyres, Saskatoon, Sask.

"I started Sound Therapy because I was having a lot of trouble sleeping. Within two weeks I was sleeping very well. I also attribute to Sound Therapy my catch of an 8 lb. 8 oz. pickerel this summer! It is large enough to have mounted and hang in our cabin. We've been going to the same lake for years and I knew where the big fish were but never before had the patience to sit there long enough. I am also more calm and relaxed — except when I landed that fish!"

Mrs. Joe Bentley, Edmonton, Alberta:

"Our daughter had a bicycle accident last spring, smashed her head on the pavement, and had two fractures to the head as well as brain concussion. The diagnosis was that she would never speak, walk or have a memory. A friend sent her the first four Sound Therapy tapes, and she gradually learned to listen to them. She enjoys the music, as she is a pianist, and at the end of five weeks she could play the piano and read music, though she couldn't yet read a book. I read the Sound Therapy book to her. Now, six months later, she can read slowly, and can do everything except communicate fully. I am sending for another tape, as they have done so much for her. We thank you for all the help you have given our daughter.''

Leigh Hackson, Lethbridge, Alberta

"I have been doing Sound Therapy for eight months now and have noticed a great improvement in my hearing. I also used to suffer from ringing in my ears which is now gone. I am very thankful for having Sound Therapy.''

Marie Lyons, Newport Beach, California

"Sound Therapy has changed something very important in my life. I am 79 years old, and for many years have tried to change the inappropriate dopiness that has overcome me even after a good night's sleep. I was sure it was not psychogenic depression, and efforts at vitamin therapy to correct a possible deficiency have been to no avail. Now, in the 4 months of listening to Sound Therapy day after day, foggy bottom has cleared almost completely and I am enjoying unaccustomed alertness and vivacity in all my waking hours. As far as I can tell, there was no sudden dramatic breakthrough, but I am grateful for whatever happened.''

Mary Ann Scherr, Yorkton, Sask.:

"My son Aaron, aged 10, was diagnosed as Attention Deficit Disorder, formally Hyperkinetic Syndrome. In December of 1985 I read about Sound Therapy and the possibilities of this helping hyperactive children. We purchased the tapes at Easter and Aaron started therapy on April 7, 1986. A week and a half later, at a teacher interview, his teacher remarked that he was so much more calm and pleasant. She said, "I had my first decent religion class because Aaron didn't butt in and interrupt. Is he on medication or what?" I confessed Aaron had started Sound Therapy but didn't think it necessary to tell the teachers. "Whatever it is," she said, "keep it up because whatever it's doing it's helping him." Two weeks later I asked the teacher if Aaron could listen to his tapes during school. Now he takes the Walkman to school and does his 3 hours in the a.m. All around, Aaron is much more relaxed with himself and with others. Because of his attitude I have been able to introduce new foods in his diet to determine which groups of foods he is really sensitive to. With Aaron's new positive approach, his life can only get better."

Brandy Graham, Saskatoon, Sask.

"My five year old son, Quannah, has always been very hyperactive, with an energy that just bounces off the walls. He also showed a lot of anger. I obtained the Sound Therapy story tapes, and let him listen to these for an hour or so each day — letting him feel that it was a privilege, and in no way forcing the therapy on him. In

about two weeks there was a noticeable change in his behaviour. He became very quiet and calm, and somehow
mellow — and also seemed much happier. When he con-
tracted the measles, I let him have the Walkman and the
stories to listen to in bed, and there was great improvement in his sleep pattern. Some time later, when he caught
an ear infection at a public swimming pool, and was in
a lot of pain and distress, I again played the story tapes
for him, and the pain went out of his ears. I'm sure the
Sound Therapy was responsible for his rapid healing.''

Pat Engbers, R.N., Victoria, B.C.

"My son, Marty, was diagnosed as dyslexic and has
had special education since Grade 1. He started using the
Sound Therapy tapes during Grade 8. School authorities,
counsellors and special education teachers, on testing and
evaluating Marty after the first Grade 8 term, were all
of the opinion that he would be unable to complete the
grade because of his problem (lack of reading comprehen-
sion, inattention, short-term memory difficulties). However we were able to persuade them to keep him in his
present school and to give the tapes a chance to work.

Marty used the tapes overnight, every night for 9
months and he himself reported improved hearing and
concentration after about 3 weeks. The best news of all
came after 6 weeks when he came home from school very
excitedly and said, "You know, those tapes are making
me smarter! I was half way through an essay this morning I realized that I had actually heard and understood
the teacher. I knew the answers and it was easy to write

them down!''

From then on, even though Marty never became a scholar, his previously strained expression grew happy and relaxed. His ability to deal with Math and English improved greatly. He left school after Grade 10 and is now working at a full-time job and has no trouble at all with the math and language skills he needs.

I should add that our other son, David, also used the tapes, for improved concentration and memory. After a few weeks we noticed that his very bent back had straightened right up — and has stayed that way.''

Carol Cree (Mrs.), 2205 Amelia Ave., Sidney, B.C. V8L 2H5. Tel: (604) 656-8628

''I was diagnosed as having multiple sclerosis at the age of 23 years — in 1963 — at the University Hospital, Edmonton, Over the past five years I have been confined to a wheelchair.

I commenced Sound Therapy on June 25, 1986, one month ago, faithfully putting in at least the required minimum of three hours per day; however most days I am hooked up for four to five hours. Keeping in mind the fluctuating nature of M.S. the first beneficial effect I noticed began as early as July 2nd and has continued every since — I find I require less sleep and do not tire as quickly as prior to starting Sound Therapy. Secondly, I find I am gradually becoming more relaxed with each passing day; indeed, I look forward to my ''hooked up'' daily sessions. Thirdly, I have noticed a slight increase in energy and strength. This has been so gradual that I cannot put an exact date on when it started — only that it is constant. And fourthly, my "downers" are not lasting as long as prior to therapy commencement. All of these things may seem to be rather inconsequential to a non-M.S. person, but to me it is wonderful.

Actually, all I really wanted out of the Sound Therapy was to be able to relax — I wasn't asking for, or expecting, the moon. Well, I am receiving much more than anticipated and am now an avid fan and advocate of the therapy program. I thank you most sincerely for making this therapy available by means of the Walkman and affordable to all who desire it. Anyone who has M.S. is welcome to write or telephone me. It is my belief we must all help each other in our quest for better health and enjoyment of life.''

Reba F. Adams, R.N., Dallas, Texas:

"The psychiatrist told me, 'Your daughter is a schizophrenic and always will be. At the age of 16 she underwent a complete personality change as a result of a severe hypoglycemic attack and a fall, in which she struck her forehead on a steel file cabinet. From being active and popular, with a wonderful sense of humour, she became irritable and suspicious, dropped her friends and became a regular recluse. She would not talk on the phone nor eat at the table, but took her meals to her room to eat behind closed doors. Her coordination was poor, very mechanical, like a doll. She became unable to sleep and would go days without even an hour's sleep. That was ten years ago. She has been doing Sound Therapy for six months and is better in so many ways I hardly know where to begin. She will initiate conversations again and occasionally I hear her deep joyous laughter that I have missed so much these past years. She is calmer, and has obtained her driver's licence. She has started work on her education, with the assistance of a tutor provided through a special program, and she wears a Walkman to class. The Walkman is worn from the time she gets up until bedtime every day. She has come so far that I really cannot say enough about this wonderful therapy.

"As for myself, I have recently been working a 12 hour shift, doing private duty on a stressful case. Before Sound Therapy I did well to get out of bed and work just 8 hours and never kept a clean house. During this case I am able to do chores at home too. I listen a short time and get twice the amount of projects accomplished.

"Then there is my mother, who had a massive coronary and came to stay with me after 10 days in hospital. I put her to listening to the Sound Therapy tapes as many hours a day as possible. After two months the doctor said she was well enough to live alone again, so she is now back in her own apartment. Every morning she gets up at 7:30, puts her Walkman on and takes a walk around the apartment complex. Not bad for 84 years old!

"Now I have begun an experiment on a man who has been in and out of psychiatric wards for the past 25 years. He is presently home but goes to a day care centre. I loaned him tape No. 1 and my Gregorian Chant tape. He has been listening 2 weeks now and says his depression is lifting, and also says, "I feel alive between my ears for the first time in 25 years.'' He wears the Walkman to the day care centre, Veteran Administration Hospital, where one of the psychiatric nurses also is wearing a Walkman and Sound Therapy tape.''

Kathleen Boyd-Sharp, Camrose, Alberta

"Because of epilepsy I have always had to take dental work cold turkey, no anaesthetic. If I take the anaesthetic it means an instant epileptic seizure. Even when I did not take it, a few hours later at home I would still have a seizure of 6 or 8 hours duration. Well, it was mid-September when I started listening to Sound Therapy, very faithfully, from 4 to 10 hours a day. In February, I had a cavity to be filled and wasn't even dreading it. I had the tapes running while I sat in the chair, with the dentist working on my tooth. I was as relaxed as if I was sitting in the recliner chair in my own living room. I was hardly aware of the drill (that had to be a first). This was something I had never experienced before in my entire life. There have been many times when I had to be carried — literally — out of the dentist's office, driven home and carried into the house, and it would be hours before I started functioning. This time, I felt so very good, and when I got home, no seizure, I didn't even have to lie down, but crocheted for a while and played the guitar for a few hours. I am deriving other untold benefits. I was paralyzed about 30 years ago with spinal meningitis, and have tended to have bad falls ever since. Sound Therapy has helped my spacticity and caused a noticeable improvement in my walking. My feet were quite toed-in, and now I actually walk with both feet pointing straight ahead. I sleep better, am calmer, and wake up ready to get up and start the day. The tapes are worth three times their weight in gold to me. I had a male relative visiting, and he helped himself to my Walkman batteries for his razor, and ruined the charge. I declare, if anyone touches those batteries again they will meet with instant death! Would I kill someone over a messed up charge on my batteries? You bet I would, and sit in jail and listen to Sound Therapy.''

Douglas A. Fisher, London, Ont.

"Before beginning Sound Therapy some months ago I went to an ear specialist for an audiology test. A second test 90 days later confirmed that which I had already experienced — an increase in my hearing ability by *five decibels* in my right ear. I can now hear the clock tick in our bedroom at night, and the birds, oh, bless the birds! My family says it is much easier to live with me, since my hearing has been restored gradually. As a business executive I travel a great deal, and Sound Therapy used during these numerous trips allows my nervous system to be protected from the din and noise. I no longer crave nicotine, caffeine and alcohol as a means of attempting to feel relaxed. We have also noticed a gradual improvement in our son's speech impediment, as he uses the tapes each night.''

Susan Brenner, Santa Ana, California:

"I credit your Sound Therapy for the Walk Man with a good resurgence of spirit of my husband's recovery from a severe fall followed by strokes."

Marjorie Noyes, White Rock, B.C.:

"I have Parkinsons's Disease. I lie down every day and put on my headphones and go into a very peaceful and restful sleep. I think Sound Therapy is beneficial to the stress that this malady brings on. Depression seems to be one of the worst side effects, and this is where Sound Therapy works wonders, making me feel re-enforced to carry on my daily tasks."

Helen Hill, Regina, Sask.

"Our 11 year old son reports that he 'never slept better in his whole life.' He had been troubled with terrible nightmares. He now will not part with, nor go to bed, without Tape #1 in your program. Thank you so much."

Don Kala, Isreal:

"I am delighted at how well the tapes work while travelling. A journey that would leave me groggy, no longer does so. A great cure for jet lag!"

Allen McNeil, New South Wales, Australia:

"I am amazed at the power of this method. After just six hours I noticed benefit in my energies, and played better tennis."

Mrs. Marjorie Karpan, Keneston, Sask.

"I have noticed a remarkable change in my child's speech. The results were tremendous. The child is speaking in longer sentences, with more detail in speech. I am convinced that Sound Therapy really WORKS!"

Valerie Ann, Altamonte Springs, Florida:

"The other day using the Father's Voice Affirmation tape, I found myself ignoring the parent phrases and imagining it was a good friend speaking to me. What an inner positive response I got to that! I felt like something in me opened up and I was full of joy. And it is an ongoing feeling."

Mary Finnie, Medicine Hat, Alberta:

"My daughter works with a computer and has been exhausted at the end of every day. She started listening to my tapes, and the very next day was amazed at how good she felt. She asked if she could listen at work and they agreed to it. She tells me they think she's crazy, but she feels so good that she doesn't care."

Evelyn Phillips, Deland, Florida:

"I have been listening to the Sound Therapy tapes for ten months, and you have my lasting gratitude for making them available to people like me. I am 74 years old — I can't believe it — I feel as if I'm no more than 50. For 15 years I have been a tinnitus "victim" — I think it started with an ear infection — no help from doctors — you know the story. I'm so happy to tell you I am a *past* victim of tinnitus! The wonderful tapes have completely eliminated the problem. Truly, they are a blessing to us all."

After Word

Patricia Joudry's book on Sound Therapy brings together the software and the hardware of some of the best biotechnology available today. Indeed Alfred Tomatis's understanding of the function and the meaning of human hearing echoes the new emphasis brought to sound and sound techniques by the electronic environment. The interpenetration of our technologies and our physical being through our senses and our central nervous system may prove, in the long run, more beneficial than our more conventional methods of surgery and chemotherapy. The world-wide phenomenon of Walkman, on the other hand, demonstrates that the planetary cultures are ready to add this highly portable and versatile prosthesis to the small number of other intimate extensions of our bodies, such as eyeglasses, hearing aids, etc. Sound Therapy and Walkman technology resonate and respond to what appears to be a common need to "tune in" and be nourished by the manmade sounds of the planet.

Derrick de Kerckhove
The McLuhan Program
University of Toronto

Sound Therapy cassettes can be ordered by mailing a cheque or money order payable to STEELE AND STEELE to:

Sound Therapy
St. Peter's Press
Box 190
Muenster, Sask.   S0K 2Y0
Canada

The four 90-minute Metallic cassettes with ascending frequencies which constitute the therapy program are priced at $200.00 ($224.00 in Canada, due to Federal Sales Tax) plus $10.00 for packing and mailing. ($20.00 for mailing overseas.) If ordering from within Saskatchewan, please add Provincial Sales Tax. Prices subject to change.

Due to the cost of our U.S. advertising, American orders are kindly requested in U.S. currency.

The book is available also as a Talking Book, read by the author, on three 90-minute cassettes. Price $25.00 ($28.00 in Canada), with postage same as therapy tapes.

PLEASE PRINT NAME AND ADDRESS WITH CARE.

Allow six to eight weeks for delivery.

Sound Therapy for Children

There are also children's stories, read by Patricia Joudry, with filtered voice and Electronic Ear. The effect is as therapeutic as the music and more easily holds the attention of a child. Sound Therapy is particularly valuable for children, providing a calming effect and easing a score of problems such as dyslexia and other learning disabilities, speech defects, hearing impairment, hyperactivity and troubled sleep. Like the music tapes they must be used with headphones and on high frequency equipment. Children require less listening time than adults.

While the adults' tapes must be puchased in the set of four, children's Sound Therapy tapes may be ordered individually. Price, $35.00 each ($39.00 in Canada), plus $2.00 mailing.

Children's tapes:
Grimm's Fairy Tales
Fairy Tales for Younger Children
Indian Stories
Bible Stories   Set of six (available separately) from Catherine
                     Marshall's *Story Bible.*
Let's Recite   An educational tape, permitting the child to
                     listen to poems, one line at a time, and repeat
                     verbally and in writing.

On Choosing a Walkman

Do not take advice from a salesman on your Walkman for Sound Therapy. Read the Specifications in the Walkman booklet yourself, making sure that the Frequency Response reaches 15,000 or 16,000 Hz. You do not need an expensive cassette player, only the required Frequency capability. Try to get an Auto-Reverse model, to avoid having to turn your tape over every 45 minutes. The headphones that come with the Walkman will convey the correct Frequency Response; but for added comfort and ease of handling, you may wish to buy, separately, the foam-covered mini-phones that fit directly into the ear. When this book was first published, the only brand which had a high enough Frequency Response was Sony, Aiwa, Toshiba, J.V.C.